ADVANCE PRAISE

The feminine, when fully awakened and embodied is an Erotic Creature. She is wild, untamed and vastly abundant. She is body, mind, heart and soul fueled by deep passion and intense desire. This beautiful book illuminates the magnificence of all that it is to be an empowered woman. Elizabeth truly carves a pathway through which the feminine can rise.

SHEILA KELLEY
Actress, Founder at Sheila Kelley S Factor

"I have watched my friend Elizabeth DiAlto transform since I met her in 2012. She's gone from fast-talking, fast-paced New York hustler to embracing her untamed, feminine soul. She went from teaching women to get tighter to inspiring them to embrace their bodies and whole selves. She's still got her fiery Staten Island roots, but they've been planted in the fertile soil of her wild, wonderful, out of the box essence. I've witnessed her peel back the layers of who she thought she should be to reveal the magnificence of who she really is, no matter what anyone else might think. She inspires me to do the same on a regular basis. She founded Wild Soul Movement and has been a stand for women being more of who they are, unabashedly, through her work. She's got an amazing business, a beautiful relationship, and a gorgeous life."

KATE NORTHRUP
Author, Money: A Love Story.

D0375518

"Elizabeth is smart, funny, sexy, and so real that at times it can feel uncomfortable. That's what I love about her. Her truth challenges, explores, and ignites, all without a shred of apology. As she embraces herself more fully, we all feel more closely held. Her evolution into this wild woman is our education. And I'm so thankful for my spot in her classroom."

REBEKAH BORUCKI
Mother of five, Hay House author, Founder at Bexlife.com

"If you feel overwhelmed by everyone's opinion and the latest self-help tips, then it's time to turn to Elizabeth DiAlto. She'll help you quiet the voices in your head, so you can hear the one true voice in your soul."

JESSICA ORTNER
New York Times best-selling author of *The Tapping Solution for Weight Loss and Body Confidence.*

"The minute I met Liz I felt like I had known her forever. Kick-ass authentic, curious, open and kind. I love her enthusiasm and courage, a true kindred spirit!"

TOSHA SILVER
Author Outrageous Openness and Change Me Prayers.

UNTAME YOURSELF

Reconnect to The Lost Art,
Power, and Freedom of
Being A Woman

BY ELIZABETH DIALTO

DISCLAIMER

Cover Design: John Matthews

Editing: Kate Makled & Maggie McReynolds

Author's Photo Courtesy of John Matthews

DEDICATION

For You, My Wild Reader.

To your courage, curiosity, and
commitment to reclaiming and
redefining your own womanhood.

And For Liz.

Every moment was worth it.
Thank you. I love you.

xo,

Elizabeth

THE WILD SOUL WOMAN
MISSION & MANIFESTO

An invitation to live into, a practice, a dedication, a pledge.

I am a woman, not a lovelier version of a man.

I am devoted to loving myself in the untamed way – through cultivating self-acceptance, awareness, knowledge, respect, and trust. I am committed to discovering and living into my ever-evolving truth. The truth of what it means to be a woman in the 21st century. The truth of what it means to be me, the me that I AM, not that society, culture, family, government, religion or other structures have dictated to me. I am discerning.

I listen to my wild soul and trust her innate wisdom and guidance.

I have boundaries. I do not sacrifice myself for the benefit of others. I say no when I mean no and yes when I mean yes. I am just as worthy of my own time, energy, and attention as all of my loved ones. I am a loved one. I do not need others to be different or agree with me for me to feel OK. I do my best to respect others' beliefs, opinions, cultures, choices, self-expression, and sexuality, even if I don't understand. I am a global sister. I am a safe place to land for all life and all people. I know that it's not all about me, but that it does start with me and I happily accept responsibility for my own life.

I am a work in progress and a work of art.

My body is sacred. I am willing to have courageous conversations. I embrace my uniqueness, my power, my beauty, my creativity, my inner fire, my passion, my fierceness and my softness.

I reserve the right to change my mind.

When I want to be harsh with myself I choose gentleness instead. I honor the earth and all her creations. I am unashamed. I trust that my temporary circumstances never have to be my permanent reality. I am a powerful creator. I am receptive. I am a force for expansion, for love, and for good.

I am a Wild Soul Woman.

Take the pledge at wildsoulmovement.com/pledge and receive a beautifully designed version of the manifesto to print out and set somewhere in your home to remind you what you're working towards and who you are becoming.

UNTAME YOURSELF BOOK
Success Stories & Results

Read and see what's possible for YOU...

"You know how we read and re-read "Women Who Run With The Wolves" and Brene Brown books? I've been reading "Untame Yourself" again and again and keep coming back to parts that really help me. I want to tell you how much it's helped and how much I appreciate you writing it.

I'm having lots of hard - very hard - conversations lately and have used the framework. I was literally searching for a framework like it to structure my convos - I was reading a book called "Fierce Conversations" which helped but yours helped more. I used your structure and it was EXACTLY what I was looking for.

I'm so impressed by your strength and that you shared your story. I love that I have a woman who is trailblazing an aspect of myself that I'm looking to develop and that I've been struggling with. You're in part one of my guides. Thank you gurl.

ISHITA GUPTA
Founder, Business Breakthrough, New York, New York

"There are many other lessons but these three are salient for me right now.

1. Through my work with Elizabeth, I've learned how to gracefully and compassionately set boundaries that honor my needs and intentions. My family no longer gets to react to my life choices in aggressive, judgmental, ego-driven ways without me putting into effect strong and clear - but kind and loving - boundaries that indicate that kind of response is not tolerated or appreciated. I am allowed and able to redesign how my parents and I interact, even at 34 years old. The surprising part of this is that my 72-year old father is adjusting how he interacts with me in response to the new boundaries. Progress!

2. Listening to my truth: I had forgotten how to hear myself and second-guessed choices and decisions I was making. But through my work with Elizabeth, I have been able to tap into my truest self and have heard myself more clearly than ever before. What is it I want from my friends, family, partner? What is it I want from and for myself? What feels good? What feels bad? What business decision is right for my company and team? How do I want to set up my new home? All of these questions are now answered by listening to my intuition and hearing my truest voice.

3. Inviting in abundance: As someone who works in the international poverty alleviation space, earning money and being financially successful always felt a bit tainted. I carried guilt. But Elizabeth has helped me free myself from those unnecessary and restrictive feelings. In order for me to give back to this planet, I need to be able to receive! The more I have, the more I can give! And the more I give out, the

more that comes back to me! The energy flows of money and fame and success are reciprocal. And Elizabeth has helped me accept the mantra: Let's see how good I can take it!!!!"

ALEXANDRA FIORILLO
Social Entrepreneur, World Traveler, Joyful Woman, Denver, CO

"The concept of spiritual-bypassing as a defense mechanism literally changed my life and I love how Elizabeth explains it! Now I am very mindful of my feelings and the need to let them pass through me without avoidance, in order to get the balance I crave between spirituality and living in the "real world". My second biggest takeaway from this book is the affirmation "I am enough, I have enough, I do enough", which I have made my personal mantra."

LEYLA RAZEGHI
Business Strategist, Toronto, Ontario

Table of Contents

"There has never been a better time in history for women in the Western-influenced world to live their individual potential in the outer world and to live fulfilling, long, and healthy lives. To live a meaningful life has to do with what matters personally: love what we do, who we love and are loved by, and living our values. When those values are courage, kindness, compassion, justice, and service, we help make our world a better place. At a time when humanity could self-destruct and take life on the planet down with us what we do matters beyond us as well."

JEAN SHINODA BOLEN
M.D., author *Goddesses in Everywoman*

"The spiritual world is all around us, if we can only see it. This discovery has the power to liberate us from the source of our pain, which is our separation from love. The scales fall from our eyes, and suddenly the world is revealed in a whole new light. Behind the forms is always the great Divinity shining through."

TRICIA MCCANNON
Author Return of the *Divine Sophia*

Preface

I'm writing this preface in November 2017 almost two years to the day of this book's original publish date. I am sitting at the Soho House in Malibu. I live here now, which finally stopped feeling surreal just last week - almost three months after my move. When you get to the chapter where I share my personal story, you'll see why this is significant.

I can hear the waves crashing on the shore from where I'm sitting. And to my right, out the window I can see them, too. Sunlight is glistening on the surface of the ocean. It's breathtaking.

A friend recently told me she once heard that's what our souls look like, which is why when we see it, the bright light glistening, shimmering on the water, we become instantly induced with awe. That awe may actually be a recognition.

I don't know if that's true, but I love the way it feels when I consider it.

I'm adding this short preface because this is the second edition of the book. I've made a few minor edits and experienced one very pleasant surprise. I'll tell you about it in a moment, but first a confession...

When I first published this book, I didn't love it. It felt like a creative discharge. Something I had to do to move on with my life and make more things. It was as if I had to get all the teachings, ideas, concepts, lessons, and practices you're about to absorb out of my system so I could be available for more.

This book was like a digestive enzyme for me.

It didn't feel like a polished, great piece of work. Part of that was due to how I published it. I worked with a self-publishing company that helps you get your book done in 90 days. Truly that's what I needed at the time, to just get it done, but it felt rushed and I knew there was so much more I could have included.

Then a cool thing happened - the book was in the world, and reviews started pouring in on Amazon. It was really helping people. AND it has somehow managed to say in the top 50 in its category (Women's Personal Growth) on Amazon all two years, next to authors like Oprah, Brené Brown, Glennon Doyle, Anne Lammott, and Sue Monk Kidd (pinch me, right?!).

I started getting tagged in posts on Facebook and Instagram where people were sharing incredible insights they were having while reading it. People were emailing me about how one part or another changed their lives. I couldn't dislike my book [as much] anymore, because it wasn't about me, AND it was answering the prayer I say every single morning:

"Use me, move me, make me a force for expansion, for love, for good, and for healing."

I also heard three different authors, Wayne Dyer, Caroline Myss, and Neil Strauss, say essentially the same thing in their own way - that if you're not embarrassed by what you once wrote, you're not growing. And if you never disagree with what you've formerly written, you're probably not progressing.

That helped.

But here's THE pleasant surprise.

In October 2017, I finally booked a studio to record the audio book. Readers and podcast listeners had been asking me to since the book first published. Luckily the book is pretty short, so I only needed one full day.

That was intentional, by the way, keeping the book short - I wanted people to be able to finish it, digest it, and come back to it over and over again, like I have with one of my favorite, go-to books, The Four Agreements over the years.

Anyway, as I read my book aloud, sitting inside a little sound studio in Glendale, CA, I fell in love with the book and I realized, I'd been using the tools and practices shared in these pages so consistently and diligently that the judgement I previously held for myself and the book had dissolved. And I could actually see what everyone else has been seeing for the last two years.

Funny how that works, huh?

I wanted to share that with you before you dive in because we are all creative beings and we all have those inner critics. We judge ourselves, we're hard on ourselves at times. Even those of us who are pretty good at not doing either of those things - we still do it in certain circumstances. So, this is my way of inviting you to put yourself forward, to put your work, your voice, yourself out into the world in whatever way you feel compelled.

Even imperfect effort can have big impact. The tools, practices, teachings, and stories in this book will help you.

Enjoy and thank you so much for reading.

xo,

E

Foreword

There it is again: "Mmmmmm...." Nearly every single one of Elizabeth DiAlto's "Untame the Wild Soul" podcast guests react, at various points during their interviews, as if they've just heard about something so overwhelmingly delicious they can't help but let out a moan. Almost without fail, it's a response to being asked a question they really like, such as "What do you love about being a woman?" I always listen in the car, so I'm not watching the accompanying video feed, but I imagine them wriggling and purring and relaxing deeper into the topic.

I realize, not for the first time, that there is a whole category of women I know nothing about, that I have had no access to in a life filled with sports and yang and straight lines. Women who have mastered the conversational moan.

I'm intrigued. I could use more delicious. So, I study these episodes, hoping to learn by example. I try out the conversational moan for myself. (It goes OK. I'll practice.) There is a bigger idea somewhere in here, though, and for once, I wait to receive it. It arrives via text message from Elizabeth herself.

The Truth of Our Bodies

Backing up several years to the source herself, my draw to Elizabeth didn't start in earnest until after I'd known her for a while. Our fitness industry friend circles overlapped, and we knew and were social with each other online. We finally rendezvoused in person back when she was still Liz, at a two-day kettlebell seminar in Monterey, Calif., in early 2013. I'd invited a handful of women I thought might be interested, and she came. Well, she came to the *first* day, anyway.

The beachside resort we were both staying at was gorgeous, on the last bit of earth before the beach. Upon check-in, the staff handed you a set of keys to your own personal golf cart, which you could drive around the grounds, including to your private cabin that opened up to the crashing Pacific. After wrapping our first day of the kettlebell workshop (which was great, for the record), Elizabeth announced she wouldn't be going back the next day, that she was instead going to spend the next day reading at the beach and working on new project.

I had no framework for this — not attending a conference you'd already paid for, and deciding instead to relax?!

As you follow along with Elizabeth's journey in the book a little later, you'll note she was just starting to honor the truths her body shared with her around that time. She wasn't the wildly intuitive, thoroughly embodied woman she is today, but she was still well ahead of me, and out of this situation, she unknowingly created permission for me to consider my time and obligations completely differently, and to reevaluate how I thought about respect, both for myself and others. She also left me with the physical gift of a sparkling little amethyst pendulum, saying it had chosen me.

I didn't see her again for several months, and when I finally did, she was sobbing her eyes out at the reception of the September 2013 wedding she later mentions attending. Openly, passionately, without shame or filter. She was fully immersed in the process of her bigger-picture metamorphosis by that point, a large part of which was shedding relationships that weren't for her anymore, and again the deep honesty of how she carried herself stayed with me afterwards.

I watched online as she finally stopped pretending she was still into leading circuit workouts on the beach, and instead step into who she had become, a thoroughly divine woman. By the next few times we bumped into each other, eight and nine months later, it was clear she had awakened Shakti and set herself free. She introduced her Wild Soul Movement practice to a group of stressed-out entrepreneurs in New York, and I got to see her in action, coaching them through sticking points with a kind and graceful toughness. The information she shared was *powerful.* They — we — left different.

After that event came her text: "Woman, I've been feeling like I really want to invite you to one of my Untame Yourself weekends. I have a gut hunch it would be a valuable experience for you."

In what I took to be a heavy-handed sign from the universe, I discovered that I had already penciled the word "Seattle?" into my calendar for a fitness event that had been scheduled (and subsequently canceled) for the exact weekend she was hosting one of her intensive retreats there. So that was that.

Exploration and Unleashing

Many of the details of the weekend are too personal for me to share here, but I will say that it involved a bracing examination of the ways I wasn't being truthful with myself, the ways I was stunting and avoiding my own personal growth. As part of our work that weekend, I recognized what goddess archetypes I related to at that time, and which ones hold for me gifts I had not yet explored. I left with the tools and perspective shift to further the process of exploration. Since then, I've gotten markedly wilder, attending a clothing-optional witches' retreat, hitting a krav maga intensive, and signing up for a weekly hand-drumming class. I have, too, started to understand gentler rhythms and genuine self-care. My default, when I'm not in my body, is still "making it happen" and "sucking it up" rather than allowing myself to receive the truth, but since I can feel the truth now, I can now change courses rather than periodically flame out.

If there is one tenet upon which all of Elizabeth's work hinges on, it is the truth. Specifically, what is true for *you* in *your body*. As a direct result of the material she will cover with you in these pages, your trust of and relationship to your body will, I predict, change dramatically due to the tools, frameworks, and insights she provides.

Acknowledging your own truth is the part that is, for now, for many, so wild and untamed. Maybe someday, god or goddess willing, this won't be revolutionary thinking, and we won't need someone to coach us through the process of how to show all the way up in our own skin.

Until then, you're going to be very happy to have this book.

JEN SINKLER
Writer, personal trainer, and founder of UnapologeticallyStrong.com

Introduction

Today is always a good day for change.

I was sitting in a corner window seat at Better Buzz, a chic coffee shop in Encinitas, CA, on Highway 101, scribbling notes on hot pink Post-its with a gold Sharpie when the formula for how the pieces of this book work together revealed itself:

ART + POWER = FREEDOM

Let me elaborate....

Art is the expression or application of human creative skill and imagination, especially as applied to the act of producing works to be appreciated primarily for their beauty or emotional power.

Power is the expression of ability, capacity, capability, potential, faculty, and competence.

Freedom is exercising the power or right to act, speak, or think as one wants to without hindrance or restraint.

In this book, I write about four elements that comprise the ART of being a woman: Connection, Listening, Trust, and Receiving.

The POWER we'll explore has many layers. There's the power of your energy and *who* you are, there's the power of your choices and actions, and there are the parts that make up those choices and actions, like thoughts, language, decisions, boundaries, discernment, and more. FREEDOM, as you will see, is born at the intersection of your exploration and individual expression of each sort of power.

Putting the formula in action and reaping the results is a sweet and highly personal, transformative growth process, one which this entire book is dedicated to guiding you through in a way that serves you as a unique and brilliant woman living in the modern world.

To demonstrate what I mean by transformative, meet Sofia, Joanna, and Karen.

Text from Sofia: "By the way...worked out the number on medical expenses for my most intense year... about $11,600. Not counting income lost due to 'sick/mental health days.'"

Sofia has been a loyal client of mine for four years. She is a nurse practitioner in her mid-thirties, married, and living in New Jersey. Before we started working together, she was stuck, usually in two recurring loops. The "try every diet or workout program, lose some weight, gain it back, try another" loop. And, sometimes at the same time, the "overwork, get sick, recover and do it all over again" loop.

As you can see from the text message above, living in these loops wasn't just draining Sofia's health and vitality, it was draining her bank account, too.

Joanna is a business strategy consultant from Austin in her late twenties. When she arrived at my Untame Yourself weekend, she'd been working 70- to 80-hour weeks, sharing a room in her mom's house with her boyfriend, and trying to save money, with a plan to move out in seven months. She was feeling suffocated, her relationship was suffering, and she'd just had a series of extremely unpleasant experiences with clients.

Karen is a mom of two from Boston in her late forties who'd been living with "one foot in and one foot out" of her marriage for over a decade by the time she contacted me. In her own words, she'd spent enough money on therapy to have put both her young kids through college, and yet she was still completely stuck and frustrated. She was also having trouble finding a job after taking a few years off from Corporate America to stay at home with her kids.

Though different in the details, in their essence, these stories have a lot in common.

Each of these women already had a pretty good idea about what she needed to do, but none of them were taking action. The reasons given for inaction were their perceived situational barriers: a need to serve clients and patients, to care for a stubborn spouse, kids or parents, and individual beliefs about the duty and obligation intrinsic to the role each woman held.

None of them realized how much power they had to change their situations.

They each believed that everything draining them and keeping them stuck, frustrated, overwhelmed, and sick existed *outside* of their control, and that they therefore lived at the mercy of the people and circumstances surrounding them.

Each one of these women was also operating primarily in their masculine energy (of which they had no understanding prior to our engagement).

This is very common in the paradoxical 21st century we live in—and it's extra tricky because most of us only learn about personal energy in terms of "having it" or "not having it," or, sometimes, whether it's "good" or "bad."

Like if you slept well, you "have" energy in the morning. At the end of a long day, you might be tired and not "have" any energy. Or if you meet someone and like them instantly, you may think, "they have good energy," and perhaps the opposite of people you meet who rub you the wrong way.

There's a lot more to living with and through energy than that, though. Your energy is your life force, your fuel. It's a multifaceted part of you, and it needs your love, attention, and care.

When you're unaware of these things—which most women are, as you saw with Sofia, Joanna, and Karen, who represent many women living in our culture—you may believe you're supposed to give all your energy away and keep very little for yourself. You may also misuse it, because you haven't been taught to use it properly to begin with.

Part of untaming yourself is gaining an intimate understanding of, and connection to, your personal energy. This is so you can know and use it well, and can tap into the different aspects of it powerfully and masterfully when you need to.

I instantly felt excited typing "powerfully and masterfully" just now, because much like Sofia, Joanna, and Karen, I had *no* understanding of any of this until my late twenties. So up until that point, life felt really hard most of the time. Once I learned how to balance, use, and protect my own energy, life got better—and easier.

I'm talking about a deep knowledge that can be the difference between forcing and pushing to make things happen all the time and being able to allow things to come to you and fall together with ease and grace.

I'll share more of my story throughout the book, so let's get back to these women.

Sofia, Joanna, and Karen are women who represent all of us. You don't have to have met them personally to be able to see yourself in one or all of them in some way. And just as you may have recognized yourself in the personal hell part of their experience, you may also find resonance with hearing what's possible when tapping into the Art + Power = Freedom formula:

Sofia rarely gets sick or burned out anymore, and she has much better boundaries with work. She says *no* when she wants to, and *yes* only when she means it. Her relationship to food and movement is easy-going and completely nourishing. And even though her marriage and family relationships were not her areas of greatest frustration back then, she's experiencing a lot more love and connection now.

Just two weeks after Joanna finished her Untame Yourself weekend, she accepted a job offer with a significantly higher salary than her recruiter thought she could get, and then her dream apartment opened up, too. She and her boyfriend moved out of her mom's house an entire six months ahead of schedule.

Here's what she had to say about it: "I feel really supported at the new job - I'm part of a team of talented and very kind people. It is bringing a lot more ease and balance into my life. I know it was the right decision. As was moving into this beautiful apartment!"

Karen finally found the courage to leave her marriage. And wouldn't you know, as soon as she made that decision, career opportunities and job interviews seemingly started to find her. She has a lot more confidence in herself and in her ability to navigate the next phase of her life on her own.

Just as their struggles had common elements, their successes did, too.

As hard as it was, because at first it went against everything they'd ever learned, they each committed to prioritizing their own needs. I know you may think, "I can't do that! What about my family? Or my job?" and I understand that reaction. It's deep in our conditioning to want to put everyone else first, but I'm telling you–and I'll give you more examples throughout this book–flipping that habit is better for everyone, not just you.

Consider this: as a kid, did you grow up watching the adults around you take really great care of themselves? If you did, you might already be better at it than Sofia, Joanna, and Karen were naturally. If you didn't, you can probably relate to a lot of the details in their stories. Or maybe you've gotten better at it over the years, even having some stretches of time where you experienced the difference... and then lapsed into self-denial and operating from effort (masculine energy) again. Perhaps you know both sides quite well.

These clients of mine learned to discern when they were putting energy towards things they couldn't actually control, and practiced how to refocus that energy towards the things they actually could influence.

And this is the really fun part, which is probably the reason why this book is in your hands. I taught each of them how to harness one of the most undervalued and mysterious forces in the world: *their feminine energy.*

As we go on, I'll explain more about the nuances of masculine and feminine energy. For now though, think about it like a river.

There's the river bank that keeps the water contained, and then there's the water itself, which flows in all different ways. It flows slowly, peacefully and calmly some days, and on others more rapidly, forcefully, or choppily. Though each element is different, they both need each other. Without the container of the bank, the river would flood out of control. Without the water, the bank wouldn't be a bank at all, it would just be *land.*

This is how masculine and feminine work together. Our masculine energy contains our feminine energy, so we can flow within it, safely, to the full range of our capacity. We can be fast, slow, high, low, calm, wild, peaceful, forceful, and more. Our masculine container gives us focus and direction so that our feminine force can follow a path in whatever way she chooses–without spilling out, overflowing, or losing shape and form.

This is a dynamic and beautiful relationship that exists between our energies, and all of us express them uniquely. Every human, man or woman, has both masculine and feminine energy.

Most of you didn't learn about or practice the feminine aspects at home or in school–aspects like honoring your body or listening to your intuition or soul's voice. You absolutely did learn about and practice the masculine, though. Our western culture is predicated on it.

You learned how to push and force, do, do, do, and to follow the guidelines, steps and rules laid out for you. The school may have imposed ranks around your efforts and rewarded you for your accomplishments, which in turn actually shames and conditions your feminine power and wisdom right out of you. This includes the passive internalization of unhealthy and unrealistic standards and ideals around beauty, physical appearance, movement, sensitivity, feelings and emotions, and naturally artistic and creative abilities–among other things.

The result is a whole lot of exhausted women who behave primarily like men, trying to fit into molds that were never made for them, struggling and suffering because a vital aspect of their being has never been valued, honored, or cultivated. In other words, some of the *most integral* parts of your entire beingness have been tamed, and they are dying to be seen, understood, and employed.

So this why we're here. That's why I teach and speak to audiences online and in person, and why I wrote this book. You've been doing it society's way and adhering to the culture's demands of how womanhood works for long enough. It's time to allow yourself to reconnect to your true nature, to the miracle that is your physical body, and to the inner knowing that is your soul's voice. We're going to solidify those connections. I'll show you how to honor and listen to them, and use them to relate to others with grace, ease, love, and compassion. We're going to create a new culture for women that is more balanced and embodied.

And don't worry, untaming yourself doesn't mean you have to run around naked, screaming, barefoot in the woods. It simply means that you are no longer willing to live like a lovelier version of a man, and that you declare your readiness to embody and operate from your feminine energy, too. It means you become ready, willing, and able to develop your own personal art of being a woman, embrace your power, and experience the resulting freedom.

If you're anything like Sofia, Joanna, or Karen, you probably have an area or two of your life where you struggle. These one or two areas of your life may also be affecting other areas, or your relationships with the people you care about.

You probably know or have heard that you've got to put yourself first, or at least take better care of yourself. At the same time, there is resistance. You don't know how to self-care, or can't keep it up since you've never done it before. Some part of you believes that kind of advice is for "other people," that there may be some reason why you continue to sacrifice. And, of course, there are the common fears of what people might think, of letting them down, or even worse, of losing relationships with them altogether if you make a bunch of changes and others stay the same (or expect you to change back).

This book will show you how you've been placing your happiness, health, and success at the will of other people or external circumstances–and what you can do to change that. We'll uncover why life gets so hard sometimes, and how to let it be easy instead.

It all starts with connections and honoring your sacred body and your wild soul.

I realize my methods for reconnecting you to the lost art, power, and freedom of being a woman may sound like an unlikely solution to you.

That's exactly why it works. It's everything you never learned growing up because your mothers and grandmothers were also raised by generations of women who didn't learn to honor their bodies or innate wisdom.

I've got a hunch you've been sensing this, whether consciously or not, and that's why this book is in your hands now.

If you've read any self-help books or books about relationships, spirituality or personal growth, a few of the concepts in this book might be familiar. If so, great! Trust that if it's coming up again in your life and experience, there's important information for you there—so pay extra-close attention to those lessons. Look for the nuance you missed before, or the perspective you didn't quite understand in your previous encounter. In life's spiral, we tend to revisit familiar ideas, from places of increasing growth and maturity. It all adds value.

This is how learning, growth, and transformation work—in layers over time. When I share my story, you'll see how many times I had to repeat some of the same lessons myself until I finally got it. I used to feel embarrassed about that, but now I understand it's universally how life works. When we don't take the time to handle our stuff, life will handle it for us, and it's often way less pleasant that way.

In this book, I'll guide you through choices you can make to handle your stuff, so you suffer less and enjoy living more. I can't promise you won't experience pain, that's part of the human experience. Together, we'll make the suffering part optional.

Throughout the book, I'll continue to reference the masculine and feminine, in different ways and contexts. It may start to feel redundant, so just know I'm doing this and articulating the ideas this way on purpose. My intent is to create familiarity and then intimacy for you with your own intricacies and nuances. Some examples and metaphors will land better for you than others, and I want to give you as many opportunities for it to resonate as possible.

A big difference between this book and many others you've read before is the goal.

I have been an avid reader of books about self-help, relationships, spirituality, psychology, and more for many years. What I notice is that a lot of books are written to share knowledge, meaning that once you're done, you know more information. You could recite it and maybe even have a great conversation with someone else, sharing everything that now occupies your mental space because you read a book with a set of ideas.

Untame Yourself doesn't stop at knowledge. The goal is *wisdom*–the state of actually living, practicing, and embodying the information you read here, and integrating it in ways that feel appropriate and true for you.

This book is designed to be a lifelong companion that you can re-visit many times over, each time embodying a new part. The wisdom in these pages will help you make adjustments as you evolve, and invite you to return to the places where you still have gaps.

Gaps mean there is space between where you are and where you want to be. None of us is perfect, and you may be excelling in one area and absolutely failing in another. This is the rhythm of existence.

Always give yourself credit, dust off your wounds, and come back whenever you need to reconnect with who you are (which will be many different women over your lifetime!).

Above all else, this book is designed to be useful. The different parts will explain things and offer key practices or tools you can use to reconnect with the lost art, power, and freedom of being a woman. What I should say more accurately is *your* lost art, power and freedom, as every woman's expression of each is gorgeously unique.

Now, before we dive in, I want to leave you with something I share with all my clients about taking advice from anyone, including me. Just because I'm the author, doesn't mean I'm right...about *you*.

What works for me and what has worked for the women whose stories you're about to read may work for you too, but there's no way of knowing until you try it out.

The advice in this book is also designed for you to have feeling experiences. My goal is to keep you out of your head and in your body, which might be a new practice for you.

Thinking about everything in this book will not get you any results, but putting the parts that feel the best into practice immediately and going from there, will.

As for the stories in this book: these stories are from my own experience and years of work with clients, both in person and virtually, through workshops, events, the Wild Soul Movement program, and other courses and one-on-one work. A lot of client stories will, accordingly, refer to their experience working with me. Some women do perfectly fine implementing and getting results on their own. However, if you are wanting that extra support, whether it's mine or someone else's, don't delay—get the help you need! Untamed women do not wait around to be asked, they do the asking and they receive in unimaginable ways.

Lastly, I want to acknowledge you for your courage, trust, and curiosity. Writing books has been a dream of mine since I was a little girl. I don't need to know you personally to appreciate the time, love, and energy you're about to pour into the journey we're embarking on together.

Thank you.

Love,

Elizabeth

I.

LET THE UNTAMING BEGIN

CHAPTER ONE
The Elements

Everything in your life has the ability to shift once you start honoring your feelings and allowing the voice of your soul to guide you.

This is about creating space for your feminine being to finally take her seat at the table. And it's not only about letting her shine through, it's also about giving your masculine side a rest. Even as I typed that, I took an opportunity to exhale and I felt my body soften. The masculine, driven part of us really needs a break sometimes. Most of us have been relying on that force for everything–all our whole damn lives.

Think of it this way: if you have a car, you can only drive it for so long before it needs a tune-up. Your feminine is the very healing, restorative "tune-up" energy your masculine needs to keep driving.

As you untame yourself, there are four integral elements which serve your process over and over, at different times, in different ways, sometimes in communion, sometimes on their own.

These four elements make up the Art of being a woman, and they are Connection, Listening, Trust, and Receiving.

Connection

Connection is the thread in the fabric of life.

The definition of "connect" is to join together, so as to provide access and communication. The cause of your struggles is never an issue of whether or not you're equipped to deal with them. Rather, the struggle arises when you can't access *the specific thing* within you that will help you resolve it.

By cultivating connection, you'll be able to handle anything life throws at you with ease and grace–and drastically reduce the time you spend suffering, or feeling stuck, frustrated or in pain. Depending on the situation, you may be called to go *within* for the connection that will serve you best, or you may be called to connect *externally,* like in forging new or deepened relationships with others.

A key distinction here is that you are *always* your own power source. You can't derive connection from outside of yourself to find the power within. You can try. In fact, you've probably even done this subconsciously before. The problem is that no source outside of you is as clean or pure as the source within, so sourcing power from outside of yourself will never last.

Listening

We pay attention, but we do not always listen.

Really deep listening is the segue into trust, and requires both surrender and faith. We will dive much deeper into these words and their application throughout the book.

It's easy to fool yourself into believing you're listening when you're really not. I did this for years. I thought that because my work as a personal trainer involved the body that I was listening to my body all the time, but I wasn't really. I was paying attention to her, constantly *thinking* about what to feed her and how to move her, and sometimes I heard her give me feedback, but I wasn't truly *listening*.

I'm sure you can think of something (or many things) in your own life that you're putting tons of attention towards, but not necessarily the focused and sensitive attention that creates the outcome or experience you want.

The art of listening is frequent and fertile and something you want to get good at, because it's the fastest ticket out of hell there is.

Want some proof? Remember Karen? She spent 10+ years mentally torturing herself about the same thing: whether or not to stay in her marriage. The instant she decided to *listen* to what her soul was telling her all along, she knew exactly what she had to do. Then, within weeks, her vision of heaven was on the horizon. Solutions appeared in ways she could not have imagined.

In later chapters, we'll explore listening to your body, discovering the voice of your soul, and relating to other people in your life so you can enjoy deeply satisfying experiences with all three.

Trust

Trust is not just a state or condition, it's also a constant practice, a choice you are called to make all the time.

In addition to exploring what trust *is*, it's also important to acknowledge what trust is *not*. And what it's *not* is, specifically, control.

Let me put that more plainly: trust is the *opposite* of control.

If you're recovering from a lifetime spent primarily in masculine energy, you've likely got the "control" thing down! Maybe you're even a master manipulator (the evil step-sibling of control). I know I can be.

Ever notice that when you force something into being, it doesn't actually feel as good as you thought it would? And sometimes (maybe even most of the time) it comes with a side dish of guilt or resentment—especially if you employed the dark art of manipulation to get what you wanted?

Yeah, let's officially bless that shit and let it go now.

The only reason you invest time, effort, and energy into trying to control things is because you don't trust that everything is always working out in your favor. You think that you know the best or the *right* way, or maybe that's just the way you want things to be. Often, life has other plans.

When this happens, you always have a choice. You can rail against what you don't want, or you can accept it, learn any lessons that are immediately apparent, and move on. The latter is the act of trust.

Control is sneaky, because it often comes wrapped in lovely intentions, especially when disguised as "trying to help." You want to help people? Allow them to have their own experience. More on that later....

One last note on trust: it's next to impossible to trust others before we trust ourselves.

Trust feels like sweet knowing and inner peace. It's like a warm hug from life saying, "I've got you, mama, everything is taken care of." Getting to trust is one of the hardest things I'll encourage you to do in this book. It's funny, because as children trust is our natural state–until it isn't. At some point, we all have our first experience that causes us to realize that trusting might not be safe. Once we believe that, we find lots of proof in life to support that new belief. In *Untame Yourself*, I'm going to load you up with proof to support a new belief, the belief that trust is not only safe, but essential to getting everything you want in life.

When trust is your consistent practice, the keys to the queendom are yours for the keeping.

Trust is like an elixir that dissolves the roots of pain, struggle, and suffering.

Receiving

This is the ultimate gift of being a woman.

You were born to receive. Literally.

The anatomy of sex is another great context in which to understand masculine and feminine. The masculine (penis) is the penetrating force and the feminine (vagina) is built to be penetrated, to receive. Masculine is the doing, feminine is the being.

When I started understanding masculine and feminine this way, it hit me hard how much time I had actually been spending in masculine, how that was connected to so many of the undesirable experiences I was having, and how desperately my feminine had yearned for my love and attention for many years.

If that lightbulb is going off for you right now, too, I am sending you a giant virtual hug and a reminder not to beat yourself up about it. I remember feeling really sad, like I'd abandoned myself or let myself down. I decided to be gentle with myself about it though, since I obviously didn't know any better. How the hell could I? No one ever taught me any of this, which is why, now that I've been through my own journey as well as witnessed and facilitated those of many others, I'm sharing it with you.

Ecology of the Elements

As I mentioned earlier, you'll use the elements–Connection, Listening, Trust, and Receiving–in a variety of ways: sometimes together, sometimes on their own. Initially, they require order to create harmony in your life.

You've got to *connect* so that you can *listen*. Once you listen, you can practice *trust*. Once you trust, you are open and available to *receive*.

It's a lovely and supportive ecology, and it's very intuitive once you're fluent in these practices. Fun story about how I know this to be true: the elements revealed themselves to me after running the first three 12-week sessions of the Wild Soul Movement Program in 2013 and 2014. As I would connect with women in our private online forum and on monthly community Q+A calls it was these four things–Connection, Listening, Trust, and Receiving–that came up over and again as both the greatest struggles *and* the greatest catalysts for change and transformation, once they had been embraced.

The 2-3-4 Morning Ritual

To begin your practice, here's a 9-minute morning ritual you can start doing every day as you're reading this book. If you love it and want to keep it up after you're done with the book, great! Do this *first thing* when you wake up, before you do anything else like grab your phone or start worrying about your to-do list. The reason is to communicate to yourself that you are just as important as everything else in your life, and just as deserving of your own energy, love, and attention.

There are three simple parts:

1. **For two minutes, just breathe.** Do this seated or standing– you can even do it while still lying in bed. Breathe in and out through your nose or mouth, whichever *feels* the most grounding, nourishing, or expansive to you. Try to breathe slower and more deeply than you normally would. There's a cheeky saying, "Inhale the good shit, exhale the bullshit," that's the perfect prompt for this. As you inhale, fill yourself up with your own love, power, and energy. As you exhale, release anything you don't need or want to carry into the day.

2. **For three minutes, move your body slowly with the intention of activating your senses.** Things like hip and shoulder circles, light stretches, cat-cow or some sun salutations if you're into yoga are perfect here. If you love to dance, queue up a song that's around three minutes long and makes you feel really good, then shake what your mamma gave ya!

   Bonus tip: two songs I love to start my day with are "Beautiful Day" by Aykanna and "Lovely Day" by Bill Withers.

3. **For four minutes, journal a "What's Good and What I Want" List.** These are appreciations, wild dreams, and desires. Starting your day by focusing on what's already good in your world and appreciating those things will amplify that energy and bring in more good things. Allowing yourself to write down specific wild dreams and desire brings purpose and intention to your day.

If you'd prefer a guided version of this practice, visit untameyourself.com/companion and download the companion to this book. There's a 9-minute guided version in both audio and video where I lead you through the entire thing, including three minutes of sensual movement, wild soul-style.

Using the Elements to Reconnect with the Lost Art, Power and Freedom of Being a Woman

We are relational beings.

Relating is everything. You might think that what happens to and around you is what actually matters. It doesn't. What matters is *how you relate* to what happens to and around you.

For this reason, much of this book will show you how to use the elements for more graceful, compassionate, and skillful relating. We'll begin with your relationship to the different aspects of yourself, then move on to relating to others.

CHAPTER TWO
You Come First

If you're like me or most other women, you probably learned, through observation of your parents or your caregivers and role models when you were growing up, to put everybody else first. You may even do this yourself as a parent, which might make this section feel a little confrontational. Please just roll with it. I'm not saying you're wrong. I don't actually believe in right or wrong priorities. I just want you to be aware of all your options.

You can't make choices from a menu of options you don't know exists. Putting your kids, family, or career first sounds like a noble, caring, responsible thing to do. I disagree, for reasons that are evidence-driven. I wouldn't have people reading my blog, listening to my podcast, or working with me as clients if putting yourself last was just a noble, caring, responsible thing to do. More than half of the women who sign up to work with me or who take my group or self-study courses struggle with people-pleasing, approval-seeking and self-denial. Putting oneself last is *neither* noble nor sustainable.

I meet women all the time who constantly compromise on what they really want, substitute wanting what "everybody else" wants, and completely lose touch with their identity and desires. Sometimes, their health even suffers before they realize change is needed.

Here are a few examples from women who have applied to attend my Untame Yourself weekend intensives:

Q: What is the single biggest challenge facing you right now?

A: My biggest challenge is self-care. I am a mom of three, their needs always come first. I am a wife, a business owner. My family depends on me (and my husband) to provide for us. I have 2 dogs, I have a cat. I have a million times a million responsibilities.

Q: What caused you to want to apply?

A: My big reason I would like to do this is because I want my personal "spirit" back. I do not feel like myself lately. I am consuming myself with work, which has helped me grow professionally, but my personal life and "me" have been very off. To the point where even I am depressed listening to me. So I simply do not talk about it, as I feel "judgment" already amongst all the parties in my life.

Q: Over the next 12 months, what are the areas of your life where you would like to make major progress?

A: To be less afraid to take chances and experiment. To get really honest with my husband about who I am, what I want. To radically reduce the amount of time I spend being sick… or afraid of being sick.

So why does knowing what you want and prioritizing yourself even matter? It matters because if you don't know what you want, how can you know if you're moving towards it or away from it? It's like that proverb: "Where there is no vision, the people perish." Your wants and desires pull you towards your vision. And your vision can of course include other people. This isn't just about you, but it does start with you.

If that doesn't resonate for you, here's another way to relate to this idea: in order to use your GPS, you need to enter a destination, right? In the next part of the book, Embodiment and Communion, I'll show you how you've got an innate and highly sophisticated navigation system of your own, on call 24/7, ready to guide you once you tell her where you want to go.

It's a waste of your miraculous human experience to tolerate ambiguity around who you are and what you want. That's not what we're here for. Untamed living allows you to savor every last drop of your existence.

Which reminds me of one of my favorite quotes ever by Erma Bombeck: "When I stand before God at the end of my life, I would hope that I would not have a single bit of talent left, and could say, 'I used everything you gave me.'"

Hell. Yes.

YOU are the foundation of your life. This is so important. Pause for a moment, put your hand on your heart, and say this out loud four times: "I am the foundation of my life."

Notice how you felt. Did it bring you peace, calm, a soft loving feeling? Fear, disbelief, sadness? Something else? Whatever came through is a great indicator of how connected you currently are to yourself and how open you are to listening to and trusting yourself.

If you were building a house, you wouldn't skip over digging, supporting, or pouring the concrete for the foundation–the house would never stand.

Well, if you've been skipping out on building a strong foundation for how you relate to yourself and you feel unfulfilled or dissatisfied regularly, or your relationships to everyone and everything else in your life are suffering, now you know why.

You simply never gave yourself a proper chance. Now you get to.

There's a really popular question I get in my courses and workshops from women who have a lot of other people in their lives that they're responsible for, whether those people are kids, partners, co-workers, pets, clients, or employees. Unnerved, these women want understand how putting themselves first could actually be better for other people, too.

If you're a person who has a history of putting everyone's needs before your own and then feeling resentful and burned out because of it, is that what you really want for the people you love?

Probably not.

And just as you don't want that for *your* loved ones, your loved ones don't want that for you, either! Nobody who cares about you wants to see you stuck, frustrated, exhausted, suffering, or in pain. Happiness, fulfillment, and satisfaction are contagious energies. For the moms reading: you have an opportunity for the buck to stop with you, by practicing putting yourself first. You can be the pattern interrupter in your lineage and set a new and excellent example for your children for how to evolve into adults who prioritize their needs and take responsibility for their own experiences instead of falling prey to the learned helplessness our current culture breeds.

The biggest reason putting yourself first is actually better for other people, though is this: You might think you're showing up fully because you're exhausted–so you can't imagine that you're *not*. In actuality, you *never* show up fully and care for others as completely as you may want to when your own tank is empty. And worse, until you experience the difference, you don't know what you don't know.

In other words, you can't give what you don't have.

This concept is so important it bears repeating. In fact, repeat it with me, five times, out loud or to yourself:

I can't give what I don't have.

I can't give what I don't have.

I can't give what I don't have.

I can't give what I don't have.

I can't give what I don't have.

Just because you can't see energy or capture it in a container doesn't mean it isn't just as real as the flour in the flour jar. If you needed flour for a recipe and you were out, you wouldn't be able to make the recipe. You might try to get creative and substitute something else, but guess what? The recipe just isn't going to come out the way you want it to. What you need is flour, of one sort or another.

It's the same with your own energy and the things you do every day. If you need your own energy to be there for the people you love and yet you're tapped out, you simply cannot do it. You might try to supplement your energy with food, caffeine, willpower, or grit. But just like the flour, it's all going to run out eventually–and you're going to be stuck with a crappy recipe (experience)!

So you see, you have to fill your cup first and *then* go for it! Give as much as you want from this full place, where the best quality loving and giving is possible.

Quick acknowledgement and reminder here: most of us didn't learn this growing up, so there's no use beating yourself up about having to learn it now. Now is always a good time for *anything.*

My philosophy around this is extremely counter-culture, so let me give you some proof of what happens when you put it into action. Meet Morgan, Crecia, and Netanya.

* * *

Morgan left corporate America to build her own business, and came to me at a time when she was feeling overwhelmed by juggling all of the stress, pressure, and very real and long to-do list that goes with not just building a business but also being a wife, mom, and friend to many:

"My biggest breakthrough is a culmination of the habits I've been creating with your guidance. By following my heart, I've changed my work habits. I now spend my mornings in meditation, movement (i.e., exercise, yoga, Wild Soul Movement), making real food to enjoy at my meals, and starting to work around 2:00pm–sometimes until 2:00am, but that depends on whether I'm being productive or have plans with people–I don't break the flow if I feel connected with the work. Weekends are more focused on family and friends now–any work-related stuff is mainly reading and learning new skills (e.g., I learned how to use Xero for bookkeeping last weekend)."

"This may not sound like much of a breakthrough, but after years of corporate-think (in the office by 7:00 a.m., leave around 7:00 p.m., repeat 5-6x a week, for years!), I felt the resistance and tension in my heart under my hand and realized that hey, there is no manager looking over my shoulder and taking notes. That meant I COULD SET MY OWN SCHEDULE ACCORDING TO MY OWN BODY RHYTHYM. Shocking, right?"

"I feel calmer, l feel that I am less prone to reacting to people and situations, less resentful of demands on my time, and best of all, better able to enjoy the ride of building a business."

Crecia was a school teacher when she signed up for her first Wild Soul Movement session. A little over a year later, she moved on from that position to pursue a new career path:

"I'm so much better at putting myself first now. I think part of it was that I loved the [Wild Soul Movement] practice so much that I wanted to commit to doing it three days a week, and in order to do that, I needed to put myself first. I've always struggled with setting and maintaining boundaries, and I've come SO FAR through this wild soul work. Making the time for it required cutting out or rearranging the commitments and activities that served me less, and the more I did that, the easier it got. Also, I've always known in my own self that my body knew what it needed in a lot of respects, and that I knew, too. But it was kind of like a little secret, because I didn't have a ton of confidence that anyone else would really believe it. And so of course it wasn't nearly as strong as it could be, as it is now. Every time you do a session, you're washed and wrapped in so many different ways of saying the same thing, of saying *Yes, you do know. Yes, your body knows.* You've got the answers and you'll recognize them the more you tune in. Every time it's more and more permission, encouragement, incitement to trust and honor your own inner wisdom. And once you really feel that to your core, it's so much more intuitive to put yourself first because, well damn, you're amazing!"

Netanya helps me run my business and therefore gets to experience everything I share, teach, and create first-hand, sometimes even before the rest of the world does.

"I put myself first so much more than I ever have. I mean *ever.*"

"I used to be overly concerned about what everyone else would think–of my clothes, my decisions, my words, my career, my life. From the other side, looking back, I am astonished to see how much I let what I thought that others might be thinking *run my life.*"

"Through the Wild Soul Movement practice, I realized how much I spoke negatively to my body. The thing is, it wasn't because of what I thought of my body. It was because I thought that because I didn't fit the societal "ideal" of what a body should look like, I was somehow *less than.* I made the active decision that I was going to not only love my body, but *rock* my body everywhere I went, regardless of my weight."

"I went to a wedding earlier this year, where I was talking with my sister, as she remembered me having worn the dress I was wearing to a wedding three years ago. She also commented that she thought I looked much better at this wedding than the last (not that I'd looked bad, just overall better this time). I let her in on my little secret–I was currently at the highest my weight had ever been. I simply had decided before I got dressed that I was going to put me first, rock my outfit regardless of my weight, and enjoy the hell out of my night. I don't think I left the dance floor all night!"

"I also think the journals have helped me to not only see the big picture of what I wanted, but also where I wasn't putting myself first, which was really often. I'd go shopping, for example, and it was no big deal for me to spend money on others, but minimal on myself. I'd look at the price tag, then decide which I liked. I'd ask other people's opinions before asking my own."

"I catch myself still sometimes, that old version of me. And in those moments, I remind her that she's worthy, inherently, of all of her desires. That she's *enough*. That she doesn't have to prove to anyone that she's valuable. There's no judgment there either, no "beating myself up" when I fall down, just a quick acknowledgement that that's not who I am choosing to be today, so let's get back to being me."

* * *

Now that you've got more evidence of the benefits (and safety!) of putting yourself first, the next three chapters guide you through getting started. We'll begin by connecting and honoring the aspects of yourself with your own loving energy and attention.

II.

EMBODIMENT AND COMMUNION

CHAPTER THREE
On Spiritual Bypassing

"The unexamined life is not worth living."

SOCRATES

I know that quote might be confusing coming from the woman who's asking you to get out of your head and into your body, so let me explain. I'll relate it back to our exploration of masculine and feminine energies. You cannot have one without the other. They are a powerful team, often out of balance, calling for you to integrate and honor them equally.

Mind, body, and soul work together similarly. As a human, it's a package deal. You cannot have the soul without the mind, the body without the soul, or the mind without the body. *They are NOT separate.* Each is significant, each has enormous value, each deserves your love and attention. The lost art here is honoring them accordingly.

I am intentionally making a huge deal out of this right now and risking getting a little preachy, because treating them as separate is the root of most human pain and suffering. Our culture is set up to keep mind, body, and soul at odds with one another.

As women, we learn to place an exorbitant amount of value on physical beauty (the body). In school, the mind is put on a pedestal. In religion, the soul and spirit (which we are often told exist outside of ourselves) are exalted.

The cultural programming isn't the only perpetrator, though. There are a lot of well-intentioned self-help and spiritual teachings that get misinterpreted and applied, resulting in perhaps the most insidious offender in the field of personal development right now: spiritual bypassing.

To understand spiritual bypassing, let's first understand what spirituality really is. Robert Augustus Masters provides one of the best definitions I've seen in his book, *Spiritual Bypassing: When Spirituality Disconnects Us from What Really Matters.*

True spirituality is not a high, not a rush, not an altered state. It has been fine to romance it for a while, but our times call for something far more real, grounded, and responsible; something radically alive and naturally integral; something that shakes us to our very core until we stop treating spiritual deepening as something to dabble in here and there. Authentic spirituality is not some little flicker or buzz of knowingness, not a psychedelic blast-through or a mellow hanging-out on some exalted plane of consciousness, not a bubble of immunity, but a vast fire of liberation, an exquisitely fitting crucible and sanctuary, providing both heat and light for the healing and awakening we need.

In an interview on *Spiritual Bypassing, Relationship and the Dharma,* John Welwood, the man who coined the term spiritual bypassing in 1984, explains it like this:

Spiritual bypassing is a term I coined to describe a process I saw happening in the Buddhist community I was in, and also in myself. Although most of us were sincerely trying to work on ourselves, I noticed a widespread tendency to use spiritual ideas and practices to sidestep or avoid facing unresolved emotional issues, psychological wounds, and unfinished developmental tasks.

When we are spiritually bypassing, we often use the goal of awakening or liberation to rationalize what I call **premature transcendence**: trying to rise above the raw and messy side of our humanness before we have fully faced and made peace with it. And then we tend to use absolute truth to disparage or dismiss relative human needs, feelings, psychological problems, relational difficulties, and developmental deficits. I see this as an "occupational hazard" of the spiritual path, in that spirituality does involve a vision of going beyond our current karmic situation.

When asked what hazard this presents, he responded:

Trying to move beyond our psychological and emotional issues by sidestepping them is dangerous. It sets up a debilitating split between the buddha and the human within us. And it leads to a conceptual, one-sided kind of spirituality where one pole of life is elevated at the expense of its opposite: Absolute truth is favored over relative truth, the impersonal over the personal, emptiness over form, transcendence over embodiment, and detachment over feeling. One might, for example, try to practice non-attachment by dismissing one's need for love, but this only drives the need underground, so that it often becomes unconsciously acted out in covert and possibly harmful ways instead.

Like John Welwood, I have witnessed this in conscious communities I'm part of, as well as in myself throughout my journey, and that is why I bring it up. It's so subtle that you can be in it and not even know it. Whether you are, have been, or might be–now you know what to look out for. Quick note, when he says 'buddha,' this is how Buddhists refer to the divine, the soul self within each of us.

Remember this always: when it comes to personal growth and spirituality, the only way through is *through*. That said, my intention for this part of the book is to take the approach Robert Augustus Masters recommended: "*...something far more real, grounded, and responsible; something radically alive and naturally integral.*" We'll begin with the mind.

CHAPTER FOUR
Mind

Your beliefs are comprised of your thoughts and your language. What you believe largely determines where you'll focus the most energy and attention. Where you focus the most energy and attention determines the experiences you call into your life. All of this originates in your mind.

This isn't a concept I really grasped until August of 2013. I was going through a break-up and having a particularly low moment. So I decided to reach out to one of many friends who had said, "Call me if you need anything." During our conversation, my friend Jade asked me if I'd ever heard of The Work (™) of Byron Katie. I hadn't–yet. Once I tried her tools, it changed my perspective and understanding of how the mind works instantly. This has become a staple in my personal practices and work with clients. It's timeless and endlessly useful.

As described on her web site, thework.com, "The Work of Byron Katie is a way of identifying and questioning the thoughts that cause all the anger, fear, depression, addiction, and violence in the world. Experience the happiness of undoing those thoughts through The Work, and allow your mind to return to its true, awakened, peaceful, creative nature."

Katie's thought inquiry process is based on a series of four questions:

1. Is it true? (Yes or no. If no, move to 3.)

2. Can you absolutely know that it's true? (Yes or no.)

3. How do you react, what happens, when you believe that thought?

4. Who would you be without the thought?

This brief description doesn't come close to doing The Work justice. If making a practice of questioning your thoughts is new for you, I highly recommend two of her books, *I Need Your Love - Is That True?* and *Loving What Is.*

When I got off the phone with Jade that day, I downloaded *I Need Your Love - Is That True?* From Audible. I listened to it over the next few days. It was painful, confronting, and liberating at the same time. I was able to connect so many dots to see ways I was creating every element of my life, good, bad, and ugly, by what I was choosing to think about.

Observing and questioning your thoughts is simple and the results are moving and dramatic. Because it's so simple, though, most people won't do it. This is one of the tricks our logical, rational (delusional) mind plays on us. We see something as simple, think, "I can do that," then quickly shift to, "It's too easy, that's not going to work." This is indicative of one of the most common disempowering beliefs I run into in my work, the belief that *life has to be hard.*

Life can be really, really easy–especially when you apply all that I'm sharing with you in this chapter.

Thoughts

The value of Byron Katie's The Work is to get in the habit of observing your thoughts and neutralizing the power that you've been giving to the painful ones. It's a great place to start. Once you identify which thoughts are causing you suffering, the next step is to consciously and intentionally shift the momentum of your thoughts into a more positive, more creative direction. The best way I've found to do that is to use mantras.

My dear friend and mentor Dr. Deb Kern gave a great explanation for the usefulness of mantras on anapurnaliving.com:

The origin of the word 'mantra' comes from the Sanskrit root 'man'— which means to think. So the original meaning of mantra is 'thought vibrations:' they can be positive, healing, supportive, and expansive (I feel great! I am filled with Divine Love. I am peaceful and abundant.)—or they can be negative, wounding, destructive, and constricting (I'm such a slacker. I'm so fat/ugly/old. I'll never get ahead.) What thought vibrations are on a continuous loop in your mind? Are they positive and healing, or negative and wounding? If they're the latter, it's time for you to investigate a healing mantra practice!

The following are my two go-to healing mantra practices. You can use these any time to shift the momentum of your thoughts and break your unique negative cycles and patterns. Worry and anxiety states are only reachable when you give attention and repetition to your worrisome or anxious thoughts. These practices will help you stop that—and fast.

Wild Soul Movement

Wild Soul Movement is a movement practice I created as I was transitioning out of the health and fitness industry in search of more meaningful work *for me.* (I emphasize for me because that work does fulfill a lot of people, I just got over it.) I started noticing in myself and in my clients that exercise and diet would work for a time, but then deeper, more personal mental, emotional, and spiritual matters that refused to be ignored would bubble up to the surface and sabotage the physical effort and results.

This phenomenon fascinated me so much that I stopped working out and only moved my body in ways that felt gentle, enlivening, and nourishing (i.e., more feminine) to see what would happen (and because I was friggin' burned out after pushing myself so hard for so many years). I went to yoga, did pole-dancing classes, took Qoya classes with my magical friend Rochelle, and sometimes I'd just go to the beach with a playlist queued up on Spotify and dance with my eyes closed. After nine months of self-experimentation and beta testing with a small group of 60 women, the Wild Soul Movement practice took shape. It's now a practice that combines sensual movement with mantras and a short meditation at the beginning.

The guided meditation calms your mind and grounds you within your body. Once you feel calm and connected, we repeat one mantra through a series of sensual movements. The reason it works so well is the movement becomes a physical expression of the words. By choosing the words, there's no room for those negative, wounding, destructive, or constrictive thoughts Deb mentioned, just healing, supportive and expansive ones. By staying in your body, you get to feel anything that comes up. No avoiding, no bypassing. The truth moves through you and with you. Sometimes you find yourself in a puddle of tears on your mat, other times you find yourself breaking through blocks and feeling completely empowered. It really is a wild practice because you never know what you're going to get, but it's always helpful and healing.

Here are some examples of the mantras we use:

"It is safe for me to trust."

"I am open, I am enough."

"I am worthy of wild success."

"I am a powerful creator."

Now imagine moving your body to those mantras in a very sensual, slow, feminine manner and letting the words sink in and work their way through your system. It's a delicious way to activate the body, mind, and soul simultaneously. It also serves to reprogram your thoughts and beliefs to be more aligned with who you really want to be. To try it out for free: http://wildsoulmovement.com/try-for-free. There's a 20-minute video for you there. The mantra is "I love myself."

For this moment though, I want to give you a brief experience of Wild Soul Movement in your body without having to put the book down. I generally try not to be too bossy in this book, but I'm going to be bossy here. ***Do not skip over this!***

Let's use the first mantra from the list above: "It is safe for me to trust."

Stand up, place your hands over your heart, and just gently rock from side to side in your own natural rhythm. Imagine yourself like a wave in the ocean, and let your head and neck be soft; allow them to follow the direction of your shoulders. As you sway side to side, repeat, to yourself or out loud: "It is safe for me to trust."

Do this five to ten times. When you're finished, take a moment to pause and notice how you feel. If you weren't overthinking it, you'll probably feel any combination of calm, peaceful, grounded, open, and loving.

Imagine a regular practice of loving movement, affirming language, and connecting energy–and feeling this more of the time. That's what Wild Soul Movement does.

Mantra reminders

This practice is simple and tricky (in a good way!). I like to set mantra reminders in my phone to go off four to six times throughout the day, every day. When they do, I close my eyes, take a few deep breaths, and repeat several times whatever mantra popped up (as in the exercise above) until I feel calm, peaceful, or empowered. Even if I'm already feeling pretty good when they pop up, I always feel even better after taking one or two minutes for this practice. That's all it takes.

Here are some examples of my own mantras:

"My source is endless and immediate. I accept the fullness of Her grace upon me at all times."

"I am love, I am light, I am wild, I am free."

"My life is easy."

"I am always exactly where I need to be, surrounded by everything I need."

"What I seek is seeking me." (Inspired by the Rumi quote, "What you seek is seeking you.")

"Thank you for bringing me to this place of healing."

That last one is especially good during tough or stressful times. It's a great way to remember that "everything happens for us, not to us," as Byron Katie says.

Here are a few more from Florence Scovel Shinn, whose books I also love:

"Infinite Spirit, open the way for the Divine Design of my life to manifest. Let the genius in me now be released. Let me see clearly the perfect plan."

"I'm always under direct inspiration. I make right decisions quickly."

Once you get comfortable with a mantra practice, play with writing your own, tailored to creating the new thoughts and feelings you desire more of, or to aligning with the specific goals or experiences that are important to you right now. Remember, the purpose is to be positive, healing, supportive, and expansive. Your options are limitless!

If you need a place to start, look back on your journaling from the 2-3-4-morning ritual and see what wild dreams and desires you've been writing down. You can also focus on the areas where you're struggling the most, ask yourself what you want to be experiencing instead, and make up a mantra to support the creation of a more desirable experience.

For example, during the days when I was hustling my ass off in NYC as a personal trainer and not making as much progress as my other entrepreneurial friends, I would frequently remind myself, "I am enough. I have enough. I do enough." This would help to focus me in a better-feeling direction and get out of that comparison trap.

Quieting the mind entirely is a difficult task. In my experience, it's much easier to put effort towards managing and directing your mind in a more supportive, better-feeling way. Using mantras gets your meticulous mind working *in your favor*. Listening to the negative or wounding thoughts in your mind perpetuates stories that may not even be true and keeps you out of your body and disconnected from your soul. Mantras direct you back *home*.

Language

We talked about thoughts first, because aligning your thoughts to your desires is a really big step. With that awareness and insight, your language becomes much easier to choose in the same way. Truly, they're the same thing; thoughts are made of language. The key difference is that your thoughts are how you communicate with *yourself.* Your language is how you communicate with *others.*

Another coach and mentor of mine taught me that language awareness is not just about positive and negative wording. It's about the weak or powerful energy behind the words. Positive isn't always strong and negative isn't always weak. What determines the relative power of either is feeling, intensity, and consistency.

Negative thoughts and language can be *extremely* powerful and have a deep impact on your life because, as we learned from Byron Katie, our thoughts create our feelings. If our energy and attention is on negative thoughts, we're not going to feel good.

Positive thoughts and language, *if inconsistent*, won't have any lasting impact on your life. This is why just saying positive affirmations doesn't work. Again, there has to be a feeling state and good energy present as well to support the words to get the results. And this feeling state and good energy is what creates the new mindset, not the affirmation itself.

Another way to understand this concept is that whatever thoughts or language are stronger and longer always win. So keep that in mind when choosing your thoughts and language. Never forget that you always have the power to choose.

I've got something really useful for you to put this to use in the book companion. It's a language worksheet to help you practice choosing your thoughts and words more wisely.

Visit untameyourself.com/companion to download it now.

CHAPTER FIVE
Body

In the last chapter, we briefly touched on the body during the Wild Soul Movement exercise. Now we're getting all up in your sacred flesh and bones!

Because body issues are extremely common for women, I want to begin the chapter with some success stories to be sure that you can feel safe, open, and receptive to exploring your connection to your body, no matter what your past experience has dictated.

Paula's relationship to her body changed her relationship to everything:

"I'm rebirthing. My heart has opened. I'm full of love. I'm feeling complete for the first time in my life. I'm laughing, singing, dancing, and crying frequently. I'm enjoying sounds, colors, the air, my breath, my body... the simple things. I don't hate my belly anymore. I'm feeling great just being myself: beautiful, sensual, feminine, fun, profound, strong. Loving ourselves is the end of all of our sufferings. The WORK of our lives is to figure out what it means and how to do it. Wild Soul Movement is an invaluable tool, a beautiful piece of the puzzle."

Iris's story demonstrates the use of both her body's wisdom and mantras:

"Yesterday morning, I did the "It is safe for me to dream" session in Wild Soul Movement. Last night I come across a job opening with a woman whose work I deeply admire. The position is something I would excel at.

The idea of putting my skills and talents to use with a mission and with a team I believe in had my body screaming 'Hell YES!' My mind tried to get involved: 'it's not the right time;' 'are you really sure?' I turned to my body again and she was still saying yes, smiling from ear to ear, heart thumping happily. I slept on it. This morning I prayed then did the "I trust my desires" session. I poured my heart and soul into the application and when I clicked submit, I screamed with joy. Did a happy dance around my house and could not stop smiling because I knew I had just given my dreams and desires a chance to soar. I knew I was listening to my intuition. Whatever comes of the job, I know the universe and the divine are supporting me. I don't need to worry—I just need to trust myself. Shit, this is amazing stuff. Thank you for reading. Thank you, thank you, thank you!"

Susan's story relates to sex and personal energy:

"I'm having sex again on a regular basis. After having two kids, and the amount of stress I've been under for the past decade because of my mom's crazy health issues, my drive literally died. Slowly but surely, the intimacy is coming back. When mom died, it was as if I was reborn. This has been a very 'deep' year for me, rediscovering who I am."

"When I say 'regular basis,' we're comparing this to what it has been. I could go WEEKS without it. I didn't want my husband to touch me. That would involve energy. Energy that I did not have. I was literally hanging by a very thin string, just trying to get through every day without completely breaking down. Stress is a crazy thing, and it sucks."

"The mantras that I've worked with so far have helped a lot, but bringing the Wild Soul Movement practice into my awareness as I go about my day

has really been the key to rediscovering and reconnecting with my body. Just walking has become an experience of connection, vs. when it felt like I was trudging through mud because I was exhausted."

Beautiful, right? Believe me, if they can do it, so can you. So why doesn't every woman naturally feel this way about her body?

Body Shame

"Shame, for women, is this web of unobtainable, conflicting, competing expectations about who we're supposed to be. And it's a straight-jacket."

BRENÉ BROWN

Brené Brown also shared in her TED talk (viewed over 21 million times!) that for women, our bodies are our number one source of shame.

In my work with women and in many of my own life experiences, I know this to be true. And if that's been your life experience, this chapter alone could change everything for you.

We all have a body story. That moment when you first started to believe that having a female body, or *your* version of a female body, was bad. I've heard a lot of women's stories where this moment involved:

- being teased about her weight

- having a horrible experience around her first period

- getting caught in some kind of sexual act when she was young and just being curious, not even really realizing what she was doing

- sexual trauma or abuse

- being told she was "too big" or "too small" for some activity like dance, a play, or a sport

- hearing her mother or other important women in her life complain about their own bodies and taking on those beliefs

That last one reminds me of an article that went viral a few years back by Kasey Edwards called, "When Your Mother Says She's Fat."

Here's the beginning of her story:

Dear Mum,

I was seven when I discovered that you were fat, ugly and horrible. Up until that point, I had believed that you were beautiful—in every sense of the word. I remember flicking through old photo albums and staring at pictures of you standing on the deck of a boat. Your white strapless bathing suit looked so glamorous, just like a movie star. Whenever I had the chance, I'd pull out that wondrous white bathing suit hidden in your bottom drawer and imagine a time when I'd be big enough to wear it, when I'd be like you.

But all of that changed when one night we were dressed up for a party and you said to me, 'Look at you, so thin, beautiful, and lovely. And look at me, fat, ugly, and horrible.'

"At first I didn't understand what you meant.

'You're not fat,' I said earnestly and innocently, and you replied, 'Yes I am, darling. I've always been fat, even as a child.'

In the days that followed, I had some painful revelations that have shaped my whole life. I learned that:

1. *You must be fat because mothers don't lie.*

2. *Fat is ugly and horrible.*

3. *When I grow up I'll look like you and therefore I will be fat, ugly, and horrible, too.*

I can certainly relate to growing up around women who never had anything nice to say about their own bodies and, further, never seemed to enjoy being a woman in any overt way I was aware of. A lot of women in my family dieted frequently. From a very young age, I was very familiar with the words "calories" and "Weight Watchers," and the idea that some foods were "bad" and others were "good."

My own body story is a little different. I never received the message that I wasn't good enough or ugly, and I was never abused. The message I received was that my body was "inappropriate." The first time I got this message was as a third-grader in the bathroom at school, when a fifth-grader told me I needed to start wearing a bra because she could see my "titties" through my T-shirt.

I went home and asked my mom to get me a bra, and not only started wearing it immediately, but started feeling like my breasts were an enormous inconvenience. All the way through the eighth grade (by which time I had C-cups), I stuck primarily to baggy T-shirts.

Speaking of the eighth grade, that was an interesting year. All the boys in my group of friends decided to rank all the girls in various categories.

Personality was the only non-physical category. Everything else was broken down into specific body parts: face, legs, ass, boobs, etc.

I remember assuming my friend Alicia would naturally "win," since she was the prettiest and most of the boys were in love with her at some point or another. She didn't "win." *I did.* The irony is, I remember feeling an odd pride in myself when my friend Alex shared the results with me and my friend Samantha.

What I didn't realize–until years later–is how damaging it was to be exposed to that level of body objectification from the age of 12.

It's practically a given to get a message like this from peers; kids don't know what they don't know. I got it at home, too, in more subtle ways. Once I got over my baggy T-shirt habit and started wearing form-fitting clothes, any item my mom didn't approve of would mysteriously "disappear in the wash."

Her preference was that I keep it covered up. That's not how she said it, though, she would use the word "modest" and, to her credit, I fully understand it was out of love and aligned with her beliefs. Unfortunately, that's not the only way I took it. This message manifested over my teenage years and into my twenties as an internalized belief that sounded more like: "Your body is wrong and it's dangerous to be seen."

I share all of that with you because if you are truly going to reconnect with the lost art, power, and freedom of being a woman, your body is an integral aspect of you that cannot be skipped over. You have to know that your body is a life-giving, miracle-making machine. She is a genius. She is sacred. She is your vessel to feel all of your emotions so you can address them and work with and through them to get to a place of peace and clarity. She knows exactly how to heal herself. She is art.

Think about that, how much real classic art exists depicting female bodies exactly as they were. There was a time when body image standards weren't insane the way they are now, when Photoshop and airbrushing weren't a "thing" yet. When simply being a woman was massively awe-inspiring.

Your body is meant to be honored and treasured. Let me be clear: *I am calling you* to honor her and treasure her, to recognize her gifts and receive all of her pleasure.

It's up to us to reclaim the inherent sacredness of being female and having a female body.

A core tenet of Wild Soul Movement is that everything you've ever needed has always been inside of you. Punishing, blaming, or treating your body as separate or less than your mind or your soul is something we all learn to do, and we suffer because of it. By choosing to honor your body as much as your mind and your soul, you say no to that suffering.

Above all else, I am calling you to accept the greatest gift of inhabiting a female body–that you possess your very own, high-tech, extremely sophisticated navigation system. Up until now, you never had an instruction manual for it. That's what Parts 1 and 2 of this book are for. Once you know how to use your navigation system for relating to yourself, I'm going to show you in Parts 3 and 4 how it becomes your most valuable asset in relationships with other people, too.

It's so good and works so well, you're going to be elated when you realize what's always been at your fingertips. Just promise me you won't waste any time being upset that it took you this long to find out, OK?

Really Connecting to Your Body Instant Body Connection Practice

This practice will only take you three to five minutes. Use it anytime you want to connect with yourself, ground yourself within your flesh and get out of your head. I do things like this several times a day. It's great before calls, conversations, social gatherings, work projects, anything where you want to show up as your full, strong, brilliant, empowered self.

There are also video and audio demonstrations of this practice in the downloadable book companion.

In a standing or seated position, with both feet flat on the ground, begin to breathe slowly and intentionally. All I mean by intentionally is for you to pay attention to your breath. On every inhale, imagine your heart opening and filling up with air, your belly opening and filling up with air, and your womb opening and filling up with air. With every exhale, allow yourself to release anything and everything, not just physically, but energetically, mentally, and emotionally, too. Release everything that you don't need. You don't even have to know, specify, or inventory what these things are to set the intention and effectively release them.

As you inhale, imagine filling yourself up, massaging your body's insides with your very own breath. On your exhale, imagine that you're letting go of everything you don't need and that doesn't serve you, everything that stands in the way of you deeply loving, accepting, and trusting your sacred body.

From here, start to roll your neck in clockwise circles three times to the right and three times to the left. As you do so, continue breathing fully and deeply—allowing your body to fill up and be energized with every inhale, and to release and soften with every exhale.

Now, roll your shoulders in small circles backwards. Every time you roll back, imagine that not only are you loosening up any tension or tightness in your shoulders, but that you are shining your chest out and open your own heart to receive more love and support. (Shining your chest = imagine your light beaming out of your heart to the world. If you were an 80s kid, and remember the Care Bears, this is just like the "Care Bear Stare.") Do this five to ten times.

Next, roll your shoulders forward. As you do this, add in a little forward and backward rocking motion, as if you are a wave in the ocean. Set the intention here to open up the space behind your heart.

With that done, begin to stomp your feet on the ground. Feel the bottoms of your feet, feel the vibration of their impact on the ground, feel the vibration rise into your calves and shins, maybe even up into your thighs. Stomp it out for five to ten steps on each side. If you were sitting, stand up for this if you can: shake out your thighs, let them jiggle, shake off everything that's ever made you feel uncomfortable in or separate from your body.

Last part now! Take a big inhale, and as you do, raise your arms up above your head, let your hands touch. On the exhale, bring your arms down to your sides, connecting them to the side of your body wherever they touch (could be by your hips, or outer thighs, every woman's shape is different and unique). Do that four more times, and on the final time bring your hands flat over your heart. Feel your own love in every sensation in your body. Enjoy the electric feeling of turning her on, and having access now to all of her wisdom.

Really Listening to Your Body

The best way to identify what you really want in *every aspect of your* life—from what you want for dinner to whether or not you should take a job offer, move to a different city or marry that person—is to determine what *yes, no,* and *truth* feel like in *your body.* Ask yourself any question you need to ask, and filter it through your body to determine what wants, needs, and desires are true for you.

Knowing what yes, no, and truth feel like in your body is going to be a powerful practice for you for the rest of your life as you move forward in your new untamed way. When you stop living primarily in your head and start connecting more consistently with your body, you'll notice when things are "off" for you, and you'll be more discerning about saying yes and no.

When you're more discerning, a lot of the energetics of making personal choices and interacting with other people automatically take care themselves. You no longer show up in any situation any less than completely: wanting to be there and feeling really, *really* good about it.

The Yes-No-Truth Practice

The reason we start with yes, no, and truth is that those are the big rocks as far as decisions go. All other body sensations and details are more like pebbles or sand, and will fill themselves in around the big rocks. There are also video and audio downloads to demonstrate this practice in the book companion.

<u>Do this:</u>

Sit comfortably in a position that makes you feel solid and grounded. Place your hand over your heart, and take as many deep inhales and exhales as you need to feel present in your body, similar to what you did in the Instant Body Connection practice.

It's helpful to imagine your inhalations opening up and filling up your heart, belly, and womb and your exhalations releasing any lack of clarity. Once you feel present in and connected to your body, repeat to yourself four times, hand still over your heart:

The answers are inside of me.

The answers are inside of me.

The answers are inside of me.

The answers are inside of me.

Next, turn whatever question you're seeking an answer to into an affirmative statement For example, if you're considering whether or not to go on a camping trip, say, "I am going on the camping trip." Repeat it a few times.

Be sure to repeat it out loud, so you can feel how the words are landing in your body. Pay close attention to how you feel.

Yeses usually feel expansive in some way. Like an opening, softening, or calmness. Sometimes it's an excitement, which may also feel like nervousness–but a good nervous feels compelling, like it's pulling you forward.

Nos usually feel constrictive, and come with tension, tightness, maybe even pain. A nervous no feels like a warning, doubt, fear, or like you might need to shut down.

Usually after running an affirmative statement through your body, you'll already know your answer. If you don't feel clear though, try a negative statement instead: "I am not going camping." See how that feels. Notice I say "usually" a lot here. There is some nuance involved that I cannot possibly identify for you, because I am not inhabiting your body, but this practice certainly helps you feel into it all more sensitively.

* * *

An important question I hear every time I teach this practice is, "How do I know the difference between positive nervousness and fear?"

Some trial and error will be required, however, the conversation I had with my friend Anthony Lemme, which I'll share below, emphasizes something important. There is a feeling of *rightness* that will always help you determine a yes, no, or truth.

Anthony's share here came from a question I asked him about how he experiences grace in his life. His answer was so potent and touching that I wrote it out in my journal so I could reference it easily and often. The way he describes grace is the "ultimate right for me."

Here's what he said:

I've learned to ask for things from my bones and the depth of my heart and then get the hell out of the way and stay the hell out of the way and let grace bring them to me in whatever form it chooses. How does it feel? Things feel deeply right even when they don't feel comfortable or good or make any sense on paper. I leave my preferences and feeling good aside and go with what feels true and necessary.

Now, the *key* to this practice is: once you get your answers, *trust them.*

I'll share a story with you about how a former partner and I came to be in a committed relationship. If I had not trusted the *yeses* and *nos* my body was sending me, we wouldn't have gotten together. And while we only remained together for two and a half years, that relationship was a massively transformative experience in my life.

To be clear on what feeling "truth" in your body means, I'm not talking about whether or not someone is telling the truth. I mean determining whether or not something, *anything,* is true for *you.* This might feel similar to a *yes,* but there's a deeper, more profound element to truth, because your truth emanates from your soul.

Just like with yes and no, sit, breathe, and connect to your heart. Then ask yourself a question and run it through your body. The question options here are:

"Is that true for me?"

OR

"Does that feel true?"

In this case, the question of "Does that feel true?" is different from Byron Katie's thought inquiry ("Is that true?") I mentioned earlier, because this time around, we're talking about engaging with our feelings, not our thoughts. Don't confuse the two.

Use this practice anytime you want to connect with your own truth. It's especially handy as a tool for reclaiming your own dreams and desires—especially if you have a history of sacrificing them for the benefit of others. Sometimes what feels true might even surprise you. Remember, once your body speaks, trust it.

And remember what Anthony said—it won't always feel comfortable or good, but it will feel right. When I got the idea for Wild Soul Movement, I knew I was looking at an investment of $25k+ to bring it into the world in the way that felt right. I didn't have that money at the time, so I trusted that if this was the guidance I was receiving, it would work itself out—and it did. More on that in the next chapter!

The foundations covered in this chapter are what you'll practice over time. Soon, you'll notice you are better and better at discerning, without straining to do it. Eventually you won't even have to ask yourself the questions, you'll just know. This kind of access to your own inner wisdom is integral to the art, power, and freedom of being a woman.

CHAPTER SIX
My Story and Soul Connection

"Never ask permission to express your soul's desire."

I saved my personal story about how I used the elements of untaming yourself in my *own* life, long before I named them or reverse-engineered my process to help other women do it, because now that you have some context, you'll be able to better see it in action.

For many years, I had an aching desire that I couldn't identify inside of me. At times, I thought it was for the love of a partner, but that wasn't it. I finally realized it was to know myself intimately–and truly, deeply love myself. This is real freedom and power, not that which is externally defined by culture, but internally defined and derived from our own bodies, hearts, and souls.

Home is not a place. Everything we've ever needed has always been inside of us. Every woman deserves to feel this deep love, peace, calm, joy, pleasure, power, and adoration within. There's not a single *thing* we need to be happy, prosperous, loved, fulfilled, or anything else that we weren't born with. The issue is not whether we're properly equipped, but whether we can access everything within ourselves and then have the faith and courage to use it.

How I Came Home to Myself

It was February, 2011.

Just before I took off my dress and walked into the bedroom, I remember thinking, "I can't believe I'm about to get naked in front of people I've never met. *Who am I?*"

Getting naked with strangers wasn't as scary as I thought it would be. Making that choice started a 32-month initiation into fully answering the question I posed to myself before I entered that room: "Who am I?"

I wrote a blog in October, 2013 about the experience called "Getting Naked and Falling in Love." In it I shared this quote, as captured from Teri Degler:

Even of all those women who are comfortable with emotions, very few are comfortable with the feeling of wild, surging power... the trick is to realize that we do indeed embody this power and then to become comfortable with the way this feels. We need, in other words, to come to a place where we can sit and quietly hold this great power in our bellies.

* * *

I'm coming to this place and I'd love for you to join me.

As I write this chapter, I'd like to change that invitation to a declaration. I'm *now at* "this place," and if you're reading this book, *it's time* for you to join me!

You're probably wondering why I was getting naked with strangers. Here it is:

On the first retreat for Marie Forleo's Adventure Mastermind (a business mastermind event for women entrepreneurs), our surprise adventure was a boudoir photo shoot. This was *not* something most of us were comfortable with, which was exactly why it was *so* magical. When we got our photos, there was one that I loved *so much*. I couldn't really express why at the time, but now I know it's because it was the visual embodiment of feeling wildly feminine, free, and connected. I wanted to blog about the experience, but I knew my mom would flip out if I posted a photo of my half-naked self on the internet without giving her a heads-up. The conversation turned into a battle that lasted a few days, and then I gave in. I didn't post the picture, or blog about the experience, until 32 months later! The way that made me feel reminds me of a quote from Rainier Rilke: "I want to unfold. I don't want to stay folded anywhere, because where I am folded, there I am a lie."

In making the choice to honor my mother's needs above my own, I launched myself into a period of struggle that, at some points, I really wasn't sure I'd ever make it out of.

Here's what some of that looked like:

In May 2011, I moved from Washington, DC, to New York City, and signed a lease to pay an extra $750 per month, which I really couldn't afford. I was borrowing money from my mom all the time, and deepening my shame over not being successful.

I felt like I was sitting on a mountain of infinite potential with no idea what to do or how to use it. This felt like a personal hell. I had such a desire help people, I knew I was smart, and I cared so much—but I wasn't making any major progress. To make matters worse, I had a lot of entrepreneur friends who were making *lots* of progress. Some of whom started their businesses at the same time or after I started mine. The thought, "What's wrong with me?" was my constant companion during this time.

By April, 2012, I was still personal training at a boutique studio in New York to help pay my bills while I built my online business. I didn't get along with the studio owner, John. I'm a very right-brained, creative, intuitive person. It was never my style, in all the years I'd been personal training, to make really detailed, specific plans for clients. And my approach had always worked for my clients.

John would force me to pre-write out all of my programs every week so he could review them individually with me. It was like *torture*. And he wasn't nice about it when he didn't think my programs were good enough. Which was every friggin' week. And every week, I would think about quitting, but honestly, I couldn't afford to.

What finally tipped me over the edge into quitting was a video shoot for marieclaire.com. Someone from Marie Claire's website had reached out to the studio about having me create a video to demonstrate some exercises from a class I'd created.

John hired a film crew, plus hair and makeup, for the shoot so it would look extra professional, which made sense. The problem was, they put so much makeup on my face that you couldn't even see my freckles. They blew out my curly hair, pinned it half up and half down (a style I would never choose myself for a workout), loaded me up with lip gloss (again, a choice I wouldn't make for sweating at the gym), and worst of all, painted contour lines on my stomach to make my abs look better.

At that point, I was in the best shape I'd ever been in. I had my own abs, dammit! But it wasn't good enough for the media–and that's when it hit me. I wasn't helping a problem with this shoot, I was *part of* the problem. Once again, I was agreeing to being folded. Even though my intentions were good, I was ultimately contributing to the very kind of subtle messaging I didn't believe in!

By some stroke of grace, the video took longer to edit than expected, and we missed the deadline to submit it. It never ended up on marieclaire.com. I took that as a message from the Divine saying, "We'll let you off the hook for this one, but it's time to make some changes. We won't always be this nice!"

So I quit being a personal trainer.

I knew it was the right choice to quit, and like Anthony said in the last chapter, it felt true and necessary, but it certainly didn't feel comfortable. The whole, "leap and the net will appear" thing is true, but the net doesn't always appear right away.

* * *

January, 2013.

After Hurricane Sandy swept through and destroyed a lot of the neighborhood I'd been living in, it didn't feel good to live there anymore. The guy I was dating was really missing his hometown of Laguna Beach, CA.

So I made another big decision, and moved across the country. For the first five weeks, we stayed at his parents' house. For anyone who's ever lived in their partner's parents' house or even spent a few weeks there, you know this isn't cute. This was actually the beginning of the end of our relationship, although we didn't know it and we dragged it out until August.

Though we'd debated moving in together, we decided to get our own places (a huge blessing in disguise, as it turned out). And once again, I signed myself up for rent I couldn't afford: in this case, $1850 a month for a beachfront apartment.

If you're thinking that I was a complete disaster with money all those years, you're right. In my twenties, money was basically the true indicator of how I was actually handling life. At the time I didn't see it that way, but I do now.

I was stubborn and delusional, and grossly misusing some of the spiritual new age wisdom I'd been collecting in books (bypassing!). I thought getting that apartment was a demonstration of faith, and would cause everything else to fall into place around it to support me. *False.*

When you're constantly stressed and worried, that's the primary energy you're living in. It's nearly impossible to attract wanted opportunities, and it's guaranteed you'll attract more similar experiences.

This is something I'll talk about in Chapter 7. Briefly, the reason I kept creating the same issues over and over was that I was constantly saying *yes* to things I had no business saying yes to, and suffering the consequences. I did this over and over because I was strictly making decisions based on my thoughts, other people's advice, and comparing myself to others—without checking in with my body.

Had I checked in with *me*, not only would I have felt every *no* in my body, I would have had the opportunity to trust it, make different choices, and save myself a ton of stress.

The impetus to finally stop repeating these patterns came in the last week of August, 2013. I was supposed to go on a trip with my ex (who wasn't my ex yet) to visit friends and go to a concert. I decided not to go, and we decided it was a good week to take some space from each other and evaluate whether or not we were going to stay in the relationship. There are times in life when even the most fiercely independent of us find ourselves facing the feeling that "there's no way I can possibly do this on my own."

Though usually painful, these are actually great times, because we're not meant to navigate this crazy earth experience solo. I was feeling lonely and sad and asked myself, "How did I get to this place?" I decided to take a trip after all, but mine was a road trip up to Santa Barbara to visit my friends. This was how I thought I would solve my "being alone" problem.

I would soon find out this wasn't what Life had in mind. Whether or not you believe in God, spirit guides, or guardian angels is none of my business—and you're welcome here, no matter what. I believe in all of those things, and was desiring to learn how to better communicate with them, so I downloaded Sonia Choquette's *Ask Your Guides* on Audible for my road trip.

With traffic, my two-and-a-half-hour trip turned into four. I knew the whole time it was because I needed this time with the book, so I sat calmly in my Mini Cooper on Highway 101 and I listened. My heart was heavy; I cried many times. As I did, I kept opening my heart to this new source of love and guidance. I learned how to ask for guidance and be specific about it—and which energies to call on for various things. For the very first time, I felt truly, deeply surrounded by this divine love and guidance I'd always questioned.

I realized during that weekend that I'd never be alone again. On my way back from Santa Barbara the next day, I stopped off in Malibu. Years ago, a friend had driven me through Malibu and I fell in love with it. I had even dreamed about living there some day. It felt totally serendipitous to be there, that weekend, with my life in flux, having no idea what things were going to look like in the next few weeks. I laid on the beach for a bit, continued listening to *Ask Your Guides*, put my toes in the ocean, and went for a walk.

I breathed in the air, took in the sounds, and looked around at the beautiful homes, wondering what the people who lived in them *do*. At this time, it wasn't just my relationship that was up in the air, it was also my business. I'd been feeling restless, like I wanted to do something more meaningful. I was over "health and fitness," but not really clear on how to transition into something else or what that might be.

I started thinking about how I'd been working so hard for so many years and didn't have much to show for it in the physical world. I knew intuitively that it was connected to my lack of passion for my work.

Then I remembered a story about Marie Forleo. Marie had wanted a brownstone in Manhattan's West Village, and at the time, as she realized later, she just wasn't willing to do whatever it would take to get it. I realized how long I'd been operating like that too, not prepared to do whatever it would take to get what I want.

I knew this was largely due to *not knowing* exactly what I wanted. So as I walked on the beach, staring up at those beautiful beach homes, I decided it was OK to not know what I wanted to do with my life just yet. I got clear on one thing I did want: a beach house. I let that be the symbol for something I could hold a deep desire for in my life, one that would even represent having figured out the rest of the details. So, using my brand new cosmic communication skills, I let God, my angels, and my highest vibration spirit guides know that I was finally willing to do whatever it takes to get it. I told them I'd be looking, listening, and feeling for their guidance, and thanked them profusely for their love and assistance.

The first place they led me was straight home to my sacred body. I ended the relationship with my then-boyfriend a few days later.

In her book *Finding Your Way in a Wild New World*, Martha Beck talks about phases of human metamorphosis, one of which is dissolving into what she calls human soup (aka death and rebirth). She describes it like this:

Any transition serious enough to alter your definition of self will require not just small adjustments in your way of living and thinking but a full-on metamorphosis. I don't know if this is emotionally stressful for caterpillars, but for humans it can be hell on wheels.

That was me in September, 2013. So much of who I used to be was "dying" in order to create space for what I wanted to be. Intellectually, I knew there wasn't anything wrong with me, but emotionally it didn't feel that way. For the first time ever, I decided to let myself feel all of it.

I didn't numb, run, stuff, or succumb to coping mechanisms like food or alcohol. But I did pray, meditate, and rest a lot. So often when going through break-ups, the advice you receive is to *distract* yourself. I did the opposite. I sat in every layer of sadness and grief. Of feeling abandoned, of mourning the loss of a best friend and the life I thought we'd create, of moving across the country to end up alone in a town where I didn't know anyone else.

Don't confuse this with feeling sorry for myself. This wasn't about that. This was me saying to myself, *I trust that I am exactly where I need to be. It's my job to feel through it and let why this is happening reveal itself to me in due time.*

Something I talk about often with clients and in workshops is the question, "Why is this happening to me?"

There are two places from which to ask that. The *victim place*, where we seek to blame and justify, whether to ourselves or others, and attribute our situation to external circumstances. Or the *curious place,* where we seek to grow and learn so as not to repeat this again. The curious place requires a lot of surrender.

Surrender, in this context, doesn't mean giving up. It means relinquishing the need for control and even understanding, and creating space for grace to do her thing.

One of the things I surrendered was the feeling that I had to navigate everything by myself. In the past, I'd taken a lot of pride in being independent, strong, tough, and not needing help from anybody. As a result, one of the survival skills I developed was to either stuff my real feelings–or talk myself out of them.

To interrupt my own patterns, I decided to ask for help. I reached out to people who said, "Call me if you need anything," and I let them be there for me. I also hired a coach.

My objective in seeking that coaching was to deeply trust myself, step into the fullness of my power, and own who I really am. I also wanted to work on my ability to stay with short-term boredom or pain on behalf of creating long-term pleasure, alignment, and stability.

One of the best things I did during this time was to let myself off the hook of "productivity." If I wanted to watch seven episodes of "Alias" on Netflix, I did. I just kept checking in to see if I was numbing. There's a big difference between numbing and resting, and I let myself rest like crazy.

Processing emotions is a bodily function like anything else. Without rest, it takes longer. The two lasting results that came out of this choice were:

1. All emotion now moves through me much faster.

2. I value play, rest, and integration as part of my work and creative process. They're not a luxury or an indulgence, they're essential.

I do want to pause here and acknowledge the tremendous advantage of being a single woman with no family obligations or a full-time traditional job to report to during this time, in case you're reading and thinking, "Easy for you to choose this path!" You are right.

What's also true is that I've had many clients over the years with families and full-time jobs who I've guided through similar processes. Anyone can and will make *anything* work when they are truly dedicated to creating change and transformation in their life. There are ways to fit this kind of processing into any lifestyle.

By mid-September of 2013, I took some time away from Laguna Beach. I went to the East Coast to speak at an event, celebrate my 30th birthday, and catch up with friends and family. During part of the trip, I found myself in a filthy Airbnb on the Upper West Side of NYC, I left a pair of shoes in a taxi, forgot my wallet at a wedding in Queens, and–after one too many tequila shots at that wedding–sent my ex a few lengthy and mean text messages.

Ugly, but true. I'd held in a lot of frustrated emotions in that relationship.

Amidst all of that, I also had the initial idea for what would become Wild Soul Movement, so it wasn't all bad. In fact, there was quite a bit of magic in the mess.

* * *

Who I am now, and how I live now, is completely different from what I could have envisioned during that tough time of transition–and it's all because I gave myself permission to be myself. I prioritized connecting to my body, practiced listening to her every day, and am constantly recommitting myself to unwavering trust in her wisdom.

I'm way more prosperous now and much better with my money, partly because I'm finally doing work I enjoy and actually applying all my gifts and potential, but mostly because I let my body guide me now. I no longer place all of my power at the altar of external validation.

I rarely override my intuition with my logical mind anymore, and I'm always guided exactly where I need to be. My life feels much easier than it used to be. I experience far less suffering and heaps more joy, love, grace, connection, adventure and fulfillment. And, my relationships are more aligned with who I am as well as my goals, dreams, and desires.

* * *

This is why I want to help you create your own reconnection story in the coming chapters. Your path may not mirror mine very closely, or maybe it does. If you're experiencing the pain of not being yourself, putting everyone else's needs and ideas of how things should be ahead of your own, constantly living in states of stress, anxiety, worry, or illness, and/or feeling out of control or unfulfilled in one or more areas of your life—my story is more evidence that it doesn't have to be that way.

Now let's turn to you. Specifically, your soul self.

The soul self is the part of you that is connected to a force that's much easier to feel than it is to describe or name. Some may call this "essence" or "intuition." Depending on what you believe in, you may experience this as connectedness to a Divine source like God, or the Universe. Or maybe you feel it most when you're in nature, around children, or animals, watching a sunset or staring at the stars.

It's the deepest, truest part of who you are, the part that knows there is more to you than just your physical body and your meticulous mind. Just because it's there, doesn't guarantee you'll always feel it.

Maybe you've got practices and years under your belt of connecting to your soul. If that's the case, enjoy this section in whatever context aligns with your personal beliefs.

If you don't have much experience feeling or communing with your soul though, it's totally okay. I didn't either, until just a few years ago, and it's certainly not required to get a lot out of this section of the book.

For most of my life, even though I was part of a religion, I didn't have the deep, *felt* experience of my own soul. Everything presented to me was in relation to a God I was told lived in Heaven, which, when I was little, I assumed meant in the sky between some clouds. But when I looked up there, I never saw him, and when I rode in airplanes, I still didn't see him. And at that young age, since I didn't see him, I certainly couldn't feel him.

From the age of two, I imagined that the God of my training looked like Mr. Clean minus the earring, wore a short-sleeved brown, orange, and black v-neck T-shirt not entirely like Charlie Brown's, and black pants. In my mind's eye he was always smiling, but he also had a whole bunch of rules I was supposed to follow or I'd get in trouble.

While I had a great visual on the guy, I can't really say I felt connected to him. I was always curious, and I talked to him most nights before I went to bed. The year I was four, I talked to him even more because I really wanted a baby brother, and assumed God would be the one to decide whether or not I got him.

I did end up getting a baby brother, so even though I still didn't really understand how God worked, I was down with the mystery and always believed.

As you can see, my perception of all things Divine was that they existed outside of me, *not within me.* This was how the tamed years of my relationship to my soul went.

The untamed version evolved once I discovered that Divinity exists within me, in my own soul. My soul self-dwells right in the center of my own heart. Even when I'm not actively paying attention to her or feeling into her, she never, ever leaves me. There's not a single place outside of myself I can possibly reach to find her because again, she's not out there. *She's in here.*

This is why we walked through *body connection* before *soul connection.* Your body's unique language of sensations and feelings is how your soul self-communicates with you. Once you're tuned in to the way your body gives you messages, you can access your soul whenever you want.

This is one of the most powerful arts of being a woman. Men, of course, can feel into and connect to their souls as well, it's just naturally much easier for us.

In fact, in a podcast interview with my friend Andy Drish about relationships, he shared that one of his favorite things about women, particularly his own partner, is how he could use her body as a gauge for how he's showing up. We women are that sensitive and tuned in, even if we don't know it. Whether or not we're listening, our bodies are always communicating something on behalf of our souls.

Your soul is what will guide you to pave your own path, rather than follow the one the external world has laid out for you. This is why one of the most powerful practices you can cultivate is staying out of your head and living primarily in your body.

Now, it's a beautiful thing to recognize that you do, in fact, have a soul that lives inside of you, communicates with you, never leaves you, and has all the answers you've spent your whole life seeking outside of yourself. In turn, the next big question is: "How do I cultivate a relationship with my soul?"

We'll explore that in the next chapter.

CHAPTER SEVEN
Mind-Body-Soul Connecting as Equals

In this chapter, we practice bringing your soul and human selves together. This is known as *embodiment*: the tangible, felt experience of soul through your physical body.

This is one of the steps that many "new age" spiritual teachers skip over, and it pisses me off. I call it shitting on the human experience. It's great to share ancient teachings and wisdom, but it's irresponsible to leave out that many of those were established in a world that was very different from our 21st century one. As much as we may dream about escaping it all sometimes, most of us have to live in it. We might as well adapt the principles to modern day living, instead of adding more suffering by taking advice that's better suited for renunciates.

This chapter's many practices are important, and worth taking the time to implement and experiment with them as opposed to skimming, rushing, or experiencing them only at a cognitive level. Thinking about all this intellectually will only distract you, whereas trying them will give you valuable information and experiences. As you experiment with the list of practices below, notice how you feel in the process.

Not everything will resonate with you, now or maybe ever, and that's OK. The goal here is *communion*, not to check everything off the list. The way to know if something is a good fit is if it makes you feel at home in your body, more like yourself, safe, and grounded.

The reason for having several options for embodiment is because you're a woman, and you're built for variety. Depending on your energy, mood, or where you are in your menstrual cycle or life cycle, some of these practices will be more effective than others. Many of these are my own personal practices and elements I incorporate into all of my courses, workshops, and events–so I've briefly described each one here and you can find links to blogs, books, and podcast episodes to elaborate on each practice in the book's companion.

Some of these practices work well as daily rituals, others are great for weekly or monthly tune-ups or check-ins. As with everything else in this book, you know you best. As you experiment, trust yourself to choose the practices that are easiest to stick to and feel really helpful to wherever you are on your journey.

Prayers

Use prayers to speak to your soul, express appreciation, acknowledge your blessings, ask for what you want, and request guidance, clarity, and support. I love prayer as a daily practice, and often pray several times a day. Personal note: the days I begin with prayers of appreciation are usually the best days.

How to Pray

Depending on your relationship to prayer, if you have any kind of religious upbringing, you may be used to having prayers being written out for you or simply reciting words written by other people. Being raised Catholic, I can't even count how many of Our Fathers, Hail Marys and Glory Bes I've said over the course of my life. And sometimes I still do. Prayer in all of its forms is an endlessly nourishing and connective practice.

If you're asking for guidance in your prayers, remember to actively look, listen, and feel for the answers both immediately and over time.

The book that helped me the most with this is called *Outrageous Openness* by Tosha Silver. I also interviewed her for the podcast, and you'll find the link in the book companion. Her newest book, *Change Me Prayers*, is also an excellent resource filled with short prayers for all kinds of situations.

When the intention is communing with your own soul, though, you will eventually want to get comfortable using your own language to speak with the Divine. Something I've been practicing since reading *The Help* many years ago is writing out my prayers. Writing prayers in my journal, even when it's the same or similar prayer over and over, feels more solid and committed than just saying my prayers. Putting them in writing is like a double confirmation, because you get to read it over as you write it.

I think there are actually studies to support this. Geeking out on research isn't my thing, but if it's yours, go for it!

Lastly, if you're spiritually curious but not committed to any particular religion, you may wonder, "*Who* do I pray to?" My answer is: don't get caught up in worrying about who or what it is outside of yourself. Remember, the focus of your soul is what's inside of you, so treat your prayers as conversations with your own divinity. This means that all you need to do is trust that your soul knows where to direct your prayers, and will deliver the message to the right place. Your prayers are always heard.

Mantras

As discussed at length in Chapter 3, mantras can be used to focus the mind and connect with your feelings as well as sensations in your body. Head back there for my in-depth explanation and two best healing mantra practices.

Meditation

Use meditation to drop into your body and connect to yourself. A lot of people recommend meditation for quieting the mind, and in my experience, that works really well for some. Yet, a lot of women really struggle with a stillness meditation practice. So if it works for you, great! If it doesn't, and you really can't sit still and quiet your mind, that's not the right meditation practice for you. I have a great podcast episode in the book companion on cultivating a meditation practice you can stick to.

Remember, untamed living doesn't *tolerate* forcing yourself to do what doesn't feel right or true. The most important component of meditation is to slow down and get really present with yourself. For that reason, it's a great daily or several-times-a-week practice.

It's also not necessary to meditate for as long as 30-45 minutes or an hour, to get the benefits. Even *five* minutes can have an enormous impact on any given day. You can turn anything into a meditation, especially movement practices. I've even heard of people who consider washing the dishes a meditation.

Another common struggle with meditation is that even when people can get into a good rhythm and focused practice, they sometimes still have pesky thoughts interrupting them. When this happens to you, remember something I mentioned earlier in the book (in a different context) that applies pretty much universally:

It's not what happens that matters, it's how you relate to what happens or how you react to what happens. You always have a choice.

When thoughts pop up and interrupt your meditation, you can feel irritated or disappointed in yourself, or you can simply *notice* the thought and observe, "Hey, there I am thinking again." Then let go, and do your very best to refocus. Start over as many times as you need to in order to complete your practice. Some days it'll be much easier than others. Be just as kind and gentle with yourself in every situation. Creating a new habit takes some really imperfect attempts at first. In time, trust yourself to make the adjustments and get used to your new intentions. Once you begin experiencing the rewards, you will also begin experiencing more alignment of your mind and body to get you there with greater ease.

Movement

Any movement you could possibly think of is a viable way to connect with your soul. Things to consider when choosing how to move include your energy, your mood, what you crave or desire, what you would like to be able to do in or with your body (like dance, hand stands, stretches, endurance activities), and where you are in your menstrual cycle. I mention the menstrual cycle again because your energy, hormones, and emotional states vary throughout the month. Check the book companion for a few recommendations on resources to learn more about your cycle if you're curious.

Allow yourself to indulge in the variety that is available when it comes to movement. Slow sensual movement, like we do in Wild Soul Movement, can be really nourishing. Intense physical movement where you sweat a lot can be really cleansing, empowering, and detoxifying. Sometimes intensity is the perfect prescription for connecting to who you really are and feeling out growth and developmental edges—meaning, it gives you a chance to observe how your soul responds to a challenge. Things like dance can be a great way to connect with your soul's creativity and desired to be fully expressed.

So move your body several times per week and do it in a way that feels good and useful.

Masturbation

Maybe you wouldn't expect to see something like masturbation on this list, or maybe you would, depending on your relationship to your sexuality. Many women carry a lot of shame or internalized negative beliefs in this department. It's hard for a lot of us to talk about.

Our sexual energy is also very directly connected to our creative energy, prosperity and self-worth.

Eve Ensler, author of *The Vagina Monologues*, puts it this way: "Sexuality is the greatest gift we've been given. Its energy is the basis of creativity, love, ambition, desire, life. Sexuality has gotten all these bad raps because it's so powerful."

In fact, masturbation can be one of the best ways to connect with your soul to nourish, acknowledge, and actively heal your wounds. So explore away here, and be open to revelations you may receive about your body, your soul, pleasure, energy, and creativity. To be responsible, I want to emphasize that if you have sexual trauma in your past, this practice may be most appropriate for you in conjunction with therapy or counseling if it doesn't feel like a safe exploration on your own.

Sensuality

Allow yourself to take pleasure in *all* of your senses by way of things like color, textures, soft fabrics, blankets, pillows, essential oils, Epsom salt baths, incense, candles, preparing or savoring nourishing food, and listening to music and feeling the rhythm, drumbeats, and the sensation of being washed over by the sounds of instruments.

I listed this separate from masturbation because it's useful to explore all aspects of sensuality that are not connected to sexuality and allow yourself to be "turned on" sensually with or without sexual components. Notice what your soul's preferences are, and think of her like a lover. Again, you're not seeking to please her with sex, but all kinds of sensual delights.

The way to turn all of these things into sensual pleasures is similar to how I described meditation. The simple act of slowing down and noticing what you feel, what your senses are enjoying, is all you need for a fuller, more connected experience.

One of my favorite practices with sensuality is inspired by what Martha Beck calls sense-drenching, where you engage as many senses as possible all at the same time.

Journaling

A journaling practice as a means to connect with and embody your soul works really well for some people–and others hate it. This is definitely one you're going to want to try out for yourself to decide. There's no right or wrong way to do it. You can find some kind of guided journal like the Wild Soul Movement journal that accompanies the full virtual program, or something like *The Five Minute Journal*, which focuses on gratitude and daily intentions. You can also free-write by opening up to a blank page, taking a few deep breaths, dropping into your body and setting the intention to have a conversation with your soul. Write down anything that wants to come out without editing or judgment.

Lastly, remember the "What's Good and What I Want List" from the 2-3-4 Morning Practice.

Time in Nature

One of the reasons I love nature as a way to commune with your soul and embody her is that nature is like sitting in the throne of the Divine mother. We've all heard the term mother nature, but does it actually have any meaning to you? For me it didn't until the last few years, but now I can sit by the ocean and feel more connected to my body and allow myself to release anything I don't need into her vast embrace. I can sink my toes into the sand or into grass and instantly feel grounded and rooted. Sometimes, when I'm feeling sad, upset, or overwhelmed, I'll find a big old tree and lean my back into it, imagining that mother nature is holding me. So really, nature is ideal when you most feel like your soul needs to be grounded.

We covered a lot here. Definitely check out the book companion for elaborations and more resources to deepen your personal practices and exploration.

III.

ENERGY AND INTEGRITY

CHAPTER EIGHT
Boundaries and Discernment

Boundaries

Amber's story:

My mom always told her daughters to marry a doctor, even though she was married to one and was completely miserable. I grew up thinking I needed a man to take care of me and also learned men let you down and resentment was a "normal" state of being. It led to several fucked up decades and many failed marriages for me. I am SO thankful I am finally learning to take care of myself and love men again.

Lucy's story:

My mother was an interesting character to watch as I grew up. She quit her successful corporate job when my younger sister was born and never went back. She is so smart and very assertive– ok maybe more like aggressive. She's not someone who's afraid to speak up about what's right when it comes to politics or religion in her opinion. When it comes to family, though, she would hold things in until she exploded, and often seek approval of her siblings and put herself in the middle of their issues. It would always blow up on her when she couldn't please everyone because their issues weren't with her, they were with each other.

The impact it had on me was that I didn't want to be like her and blow up on people, but I also didn't want to upset anyone, so I never really formed or expressed opinions about important issues. I also wanted everyone's approval, too, so I became very agreeable and it took me years to first discover my own personality and preferences and then feel comfortable asking for what I wanted.

Michelle's story:

My mother is a super-submissive wife, deferring to my dad in all things, even when disciplining of us reached I dangerous, abusive levels. Through it all, she held her tongue. With my first engagement (until I listened enough to the whisper of "no" to break it off) and in the first several years of my marriage to my husband, I deferred. Held my tongue, even when my insides were screaming, "No!!!

My husband bought a home while I was on vacation with my sisters, and I had never even SEEN it. When he called me to tell me, all I said was, "Well, if you're sure. You are the head of the house, so I trust your judgment." When, the whole time, my insides were SCREAMING, "But I don't trust your judgment AT ALL! This doesn't feel good! This doesn't feel safe! You have already gotten us into so much debt and I don't want anymore! We can't afford it! What made you decide to sign something when I had never even laid eyes on it???!!! What the FUCK!!!!!!" We moved in a month later.

This would NEVER HAPPEN TO ME NOW. Not even CLOSE. But I never knew any different. The women in my family deferred. The men were the heads of the house and thus, God. It was such a patriarchal, Christian doctrine that it makes me ill to think about the powerlessness of women in the culture that I grew up in. I feel ill thinking about my life as it used to be, and where I would be now if I hadn't listened to my own voice. It kind of breaks my heart, actually. How long I followed along and ignored Michelle. Because Michelle is wise, and deep, and fun, and intelligent, and it took me so long to know her. It breaks my heart for my mother, who is also all of those things and so much more, and yet, she may never feel safe enough to acknowledge those superpowers and BE HERSELF. And I would so love to be ourselves together and experience that.

These are all typical and relatable for most women living in the 21st century. Of the thousands of women I've met in my life, I can think of two who have described their mothers as women who took really great care of themselves and, in turn, imparted any kind of wisdom to their daughters about womanhood or self-love.

It's no wonder boundaries are a non-existent or misunderstood topic in most of our lives—at least until we learn better.

Whether the message comes across explicitly or by demonstration, most of us learn from a very young age that being a caregiver and putting others' needs before our own is how to love. And love is the primary currency we women *crave*.

In *Women Who Run with the Wolves*, Dr. Clarissa Pinkola Estes talks about how the two primary feminine archetypes our culture embraces and respects most are the maiden and the mother.

The maiden is innocent, demure, virginal, subservient, and young. The mother is a nurturer and caregiver to all. So what about those of us who don't strongly identify with either category? (Which, by the way, is a whole lot of women!)

The truth is, we're not given as much value or sense of place in this society, which is extremely damaging to our psyche, self-esteem, and ways of being.

On some level, we learn to try and fit into these molds so we'll be accepted, instead of *being* the mold or *creating* the mold that is true to us. This is where we get tripped up with boundaries. We end up saying *yes* when we mean *no*, letting people walk all over us, and we wind up feeling undervalued and under-appreciated as a result.

This extends beyond the home too. In the working world and in the private sector in particular, women are still paid, on average, 78 cents for every dollar a man earns in the U.S.–despite being the primary breadwinners in over 40% of today's households.

And boundaries aren't just an incoming issue, as in something to defend against intrusion by others. Every woman who over-gives or over-extends herself is also often violating her own as well as other people's boundaries in the process.

Here's an example:

Terry is a mother of two who's been the primary breadwinner in her home for over a decade. She pays all of the household bills and sometimes helps her son and husband with their personal bills. On many occasions over the years, she's paid their bills even when they didn't ask her to, because she can't stand the idea of their credit scores being damaged or the idea of them incurring extra late fees or paying more interest.

While her intention is kind and generous, it's also self-serving, destructive, and crosses their boundaries. Terry is jumping into their experience and trying to "fix" things without being asked. In the process of fixing what she perceives to be their problem, she also robs them of the opportunity to figure out their own solutions and develop the skills to keep the problem from recurring. This results in a cycle where she feels resentful, taken advantage of, and even, at times, unloved, while they never have to step up because they know she'll always be the safety net.

* * *

One of the most loving things we can do for other people is allow them to have their own experience. This means not jumping into things uninvited, and not being the clean-up crew behind their mistakes.

Now, if you're thinking of all the times you've done similar things, don't dwell on it. Before you close this book, you're not going to do that anymore.

The highest form of integrity is to honor yourself. This means that sometimes you won't finish what you started or that you might break a commitment–and that's totally OK. I understand that my view is counter-culture, like many other points in this book. So let me explain before you toss this book out and write me off as a whack job.

When I was running Wild Soul Movement Virtual sessions seasonally, I would upload new videos every Monday for 12 weeks at 6:30 a.m. ET. A handful of times over the course of these sessions, I chose not to upload the video on a Monday or at that specific time. Each time it happened, I'd be totally honest about it, own it, make a new commitment–and stick to it.

While I knew there was a risk that I might upset or disappoint a customer if the video came late, it was more important to me to protect my own energy so I could show up fully at a better time. I chose that rather than to push myself when I wasn't feeling it, and in turn to show up with less than my best. This is very closely connected to everything we covered in Chapter 2 about putting yourself first.

Here's an example of one of those times.

My post to the group on August 17, 2014:

Strong intuition alert!

I want to go to the beach in La Jolla to shoot this week's video, and it would be insane to go on a Sunday, so I'm gonna go tomorrow and post the video later in the day–instead of 6:30 a.m.

It's funny, because Mike is here with me, and he was kinda giving me some pushback on posting my video late. I had to explain how Intuition is Queen in the Wild Soul Movement world.

Loving you women and this place extra hard for that right now.

The responses I received:

"I love La Jolla! That is where my husband and I met and it is also where he proposed. Let that intuition flow, yo!!!!"

"I love La Jolla too!! We trust you mama, like [name deleted for privacy] said just let it flow!!"

"I need to visit La Jolla! Wheeee. Way to stick to your intuition :) We don't mind."

"I'm sure it will be awesome, can't wait!"

Case in point: people respect and admire those with boundaries. That was a professional example, so let me give you a personal one. The following is two peeks into the story of how one of my long term relationships came to be.

November, 2013

I'd originally met this man in passing after a yoga class during the Springtime in New York City. I wouldn't reconnect with him again until a year and a half later, first in Los Angeles, then once again in New York. This second rendezvous in New York included elements of both disaster and bliss.

The short version of the story is that he invited too many women he was interested in to one party. One moment, we're walking down the street holding hands and dancing; a few hours later, I see him making out with some chick at the bar.

I don't play games like that, so I left and let him know I was hurt and disappointed. I knew when I met him he was a world traveler and not monogamous. I felt our connection to be real, but this kind of behavior wasn't my vibe.

After a beautiful and loving apology, I agreed to see him two days later. It was clear that our connection was special, but that maybe our timing wasn't very good. So what I thought was going to be a closed loop stayed open. Really, I stayed open. A pattern I had fallen into in many past relationships was not falling in love with the man right in front of me but the *idea* of him, of what he or we could be.

With this person, these bumps along the way (of which there would be a few more), presented me with the chance to love what was right in front of me, release my judgments, and practice compassion, forgiveness, and acceptance. They also challenged me to be discerning about not settling or talking myself out of how I really felt in tough situations.

April, 2014

By April, we'd been seeing each other for about six months. It wasn't serious, but it wasn't not serious. He was still traveling full-time, so I would see him for a few days or a few weeks at a time, and then not for days or weeks. For that reason, neither one of us felt super-compelled to commit, but we did have some agreements around intimacy with other people, which at that time did not take kissing or sexual touch with other people off the table.

So he called me one day and told me about the night before. He'd gone out with a few new friends and at the end of the night, everyone else had left except him and one woman. They ended up having a pretty intimate time dancing, but that was it, nothing sexual. When he told me this, I thought, "There's nothing wrong with that, he didn't break any of our agreements." And I even said that to him on the phone. But when I hung up, let the information sink into my body, and felt about it instead of thinking about it, it was *not* OK with me.

This was a pivotal moment where I had a choice. I could choose the way I used to do things, which was internalize my feelings and deal with them on my own so as not to come off as crazy, emotional, or high maintenance. That kind of withholding isn't even an apology for being who you are, it's a flat-out denial of what's true. Instead, I chose to speak up.

The next morning, I called him and shared exactly how I felt in my body. And how it conflicted with what my head was saying, but my practice was to always trust my body and not logic my way out of things anymore. I then shared that I wasn't interested in asking him to deny himself his wants or desires, but if he really felt the need to continue having intimate interactions with women like this, I was no longer interested in having a relationship with him.

After a long pause he said, "Ok, I'm in." And then another long pause...."I think you just tricked me into being in a monogamous relationship." To which I replied, "Great. Stick around as long as it feels good and feel free to peace out when it doesn't." As I mentioned earlier, that relationship lasted for another two and a half years and was a valuable learning experience.

I want to highlight and repeat something really important from this story to remind you how useful the Yes-No-Truth Practice from Chapter 5 really is.

When he told me he'd gone dancing with this woman, that it was intimate but not sexual, in my *mind* I thought, *There's nothing wrong with that, he didn't break any of our agreements.* And I even said that to him on the phone at first. But after I hung up, let the information sink into my body, and *felt* about it instead of thinking about it, it was not OK with me anymore. That's why I spoke up and drew my boundary.

Discernment

This is one of my favorite art forms to practice. And it is an art, because when used consistently, the results are beautiful.

Discernment means knowing what is for you and what isn't. This will take some trial and error, and it will also change over time. That's why the practice of staying connected to and listening to your body is so valuable. When your preferences shift, you know. When you know what yeses, nos, and truths feel like in your body, you will feel less and less guilty about putting your needs first. In time, you will be in much better alignment with your choices.

In a few chapters, when I talk about relating to other people, I'll give you some great conversation prompts for how to say no with grace. You may also enjoy a podcast interview with my friend Alexis Neely called "How to Be A Free Range Adult." In it, we talk about being OK with being "consistently inconsistent" as women, and how to communicate when you change your mind about something or need to break a commitment to yourself or someone else. The link is in the book companion with all the other resources already mentioned.

People who aren't discerning often misread discernment as judgmental. What differentiates the two is whether or not you place value or meaning on something or someone beyond *yes* or *no.*

To say, "I can't stand that person," give them an unflattering label, or avoid them is judgment. To recognize it simply doesn't feel good to be around them and make the choice not to spend time with someone who doesn't feel right or like an energetic match for you is discernment. The difference is judgment makes someone or something right or wrong. Discernment just says, "I'm up for that" or "I'm not up for that."

I had a friend once who wasn't discerning at all, and he would constantly accuse me of being judgy. Months later, he was feeling energetically and emotionally depleted. He realized that it was because he had so many energetic cords out in the world. Then he started practicing discernment and saying no more often. As a result, he had a lot more energy to put into the things that were (and are) important to him.

Just recently, he wrote a beautiful post on Facebook: "I owe Elizabeth so much for teaching me the art of discernment." So have no fear, it's absolutely a skill you can cultivate over time. Like almost everything else in this book, it just takes practice.

A cautionary note on boundaries and discernment: while these are two practices that will yield tons of benefits and positive results in your life, there are inevitable growing pains. You may experience some friction in your relationships as you transition into holding better boundaries and being more discerning. People will project their own insecurities and lack of boundaries onto you once you start honoring yourself consistently, and this will be uncomfortable. Some relationships may even work their way out of your life.

While everything I just said may seem like reasons not to have boundaries or practice discernment, trust me, people who are not willing to honor your choices to better care for yourself and nurture your own energy are not the people you want in your life.

The rest of this chapter is dedicated to determining where to get started setting your boundaries, by identifying where you need them most.

Setting Boundaries

Sacred Seven Exercise:

Grab a blank sheet of paper and write down what you believe to be the seven most important areas of your life. Here's an example from a woman who came to my Untame Yourself weekend in August, 2015:

Career

Family

Romantic Relationship

Health/Body

Spirituality

Lifestyle/Environment (this includes travel)

Money

Next rank each one–as it appears today–on a scale of 1 to 5. 1 being the worst kind of personal hell, 5 being ideal, heaven on earth, wild dreams fulfilled, absolutely incredible.

Now, circle the areas you ranked a 3 or lower. Remember, humans are relational beings. Everything is about relationships. More than likely, the relationships that exist within the categories ranking low on your list are the ones where you put others' needs ahead of your own and can use some better boundaries.

Let me also be super clear about what I mean when I say "others' needs." These might not even be explicitly agreed upon needs; they might be needs that you've assumed responsibility for without questioning them.

Here's an example. When Alexis came to her Untame Yourself weekend, she was struggling with her relationship with her father. After a bit of time in what I call the "hot seat," where each woman gets 40-60 minutes of one-on-one coaching from me, we uncovered the roots of that. Even though her father never explicitly said to her, "I need you to be more like me," she had been assuming for years that was all he wanted out of her, and therefore Alexis put all kinds of pressure on herself to either be more like him, or deal with the sense that she was disappointing him if she wasn't.

By being transparent with him in their next conversation, they were able to clear this right up. Both Alexis and her father discovered many things they didn't know about each other, because they'd been so busy making assumptions that weren't true! Transparent communication is everything. It saves you from putting effort and energy towards things that aren't even real, so you can instead focus on what's actually happening.

In Chapter 10, I'll give you some frameworks for transparent communication–so hang onto your Sacred Seven list and rankings.

CHAPTER NINE
Trust and Receiving

If you remember back to Chapter 1, I mentioned that trust is the opposite of control. For the purposes of untaming yourself, and experiencing the fullness of your power as well as the freedom that is your birthright as a woman, we're going to treat trust as a *choice*, not as a state or condition.

The reason is that if you want trust to work for you, you constantly have to choose it. Choosing trust isn't easy or automatic, it's actually a *practice*. In this chapter, I'll walk you through some ways to make trust an easier, more consistent choice that feels safe. I've worked with enough women over the years to know that you're not going to choose anything that doesn't make you feel safe.

The Truth about Trust

The very, very frustrating thing about trust is that once you commit yourself to it, you will be tested. Over and over... and over. You will forget to trust, then you will remember. You will go on a streak of deep trust and experience all the miracles of trusting, then you will relapse.

Trust is kind of like your family. Sometimes they're so easy to love: there's so much history, nostalgia, great memories that hold you together fondly (maybe)–and other times you want to rip their fucking faces off.

You will feel this way about trust when you surrender your full faith–and the outcome of a situation isn't what you hoped for. And this is actually trust's way of inviting you to keep believing, keep surrendering, keep looking for the clues to the perfection of life, even when it's UUUGGGLLLYYY.

As terrible as it sounds, it's equal parts exhilarating and awe-inspiring and it bears unimaginable amounts of joy, pleasure, and bliss. It's the entire human experience wrapped up in a bow: the practice of choosing trust.

Pause....

Before I move on I want to pause (out loud) and make sure you're following all the ways the Elements of Untaming Yourself are building upon each other so far.

- When you can connect to your body, you become more tuned in to the feelings and sensations she's constantly using to communicate with you.

- When you practice listening to those feelings and sensations instead of the rationale and logic your meticulous mind employs to talk you out of it, you become more aligned with your soul. Ultimately, your body is your soul's instrument for communication.

- Trust is the next step. Remember, you can be connected to your body and listening to the information, but if you don't trust it, that information becomes useless. A healing mantra practice is also fantastic here to keep you focused on what you want and help trust feel like a safer choice.

So let's take a deeper look at *your* relationship to trust.

I don't know about you, but I did not grow up seeing any proof that it was safe to trust. And aside from getting that message via observation, it was also directly programmed into me.

I was always really close to my mom's dad, who we called Pop. Every time I would leave his house, he would say, "Remember what I always tell you, *trust no one.*"

Pop wasn't a guy who used the words "I love you" often. To this day, I really believe that, in his old-Italian-guy-from-Brooklyn way, his mantra to not trust anybody was his way of telling me he loved me all the time. Even though I can see the sweetness and good intentions in it, that doesn't mean it was any less damaging of a belief to take on.

My dad's mom, my Abuelita, also always ended conversations or visits with something similar: "Be careful mi amor, and remember, don't trust anybody."

Did you get that message from a family member or loved one, too? The message can be communicated with words or behavior, so even if you don't remember hearing it, is there a chance that your reluctance to trust has to do with learning from adults who you grew up around?

In the Wild Soul Movement Virtual Program, we dedicate an entire module to trust and surrender. Without fail, whenever we get there, several women's internal alarm systems go off. All completely justified, as they each had unique experiences that taught them mistrust—especially times when they trusted and ended up getting hurt or taken advantage of.

So how do you recover from something like that and learn to trust? This may sound even crazier than actually trusting: *you forgive and let go of those memories and experiences.*

Because I've taught this so many times in courses, on coaching calls, and in small group intensives, and I've been practicing forgiveness work myself for years, I know your objections. I want to be really clear what I mean when I say forgiveness.

Forgiveness is *for the forgiver.* It's 100% for you, for your freedom. I don't want you to let anyone off the hook for doing something terrible, but I do want you to take your power back from that person or situation. It's over. The event or offense happened in the past. Maybe it only happened once, or maybe it stopped happening at last. Every time you've relived it since has turned *you* into the offender, and reinforced the belief in you that you can't trust life, yourself, or other people.

Now, before you throw the book across the room and curse my name, please know I say that to you with so much love–and understand why. As much as it's a blessing that your body is highly sensitive and communicative, in this case, it's not beneficial. Everything has a shadow side.

Your body doesn't know the difference between signals from your mind. That is, she can't discern whether something is happening in real time or if it was a past event. She only knows what she feels and reacts accordingly. So when you relive scary, painful, or traumatic events, you trigger all the same chemical, physical, and emotional reactions that you would have in your body if it was happening right now.

Can you see why asking you to stop doing that is a loving request, and not an accusation or invalidation?

When you can be honest with yourself–when you can accept that you've been the one committing the act of *remembering and reliving* your traumas and bad memories–you begin to own your power and notice your own ability to choose to stop doing that to yourself. That means you can *stop* feeling the pain and everything that goes along with it.

This is huge, and this is why *trust* is a pathway to freedom. When you get to a place of trust, you believe with your whole heart that, as Byron Katie says, "... everything happens for you, not to you." And yes, I know this is the second time in this book I'm referencing that quote. It's *that* impactful.

You can heal your wounds, and in turn derive more strength and power from doing so, because this *is* how you take back your power and energy. This means you can *feel better.* And when you feel better, you can literally have anything you want in life.

Below is the forgiveness practice I've been using since 2012, partly based on the Hawaiian tradition of ho'oponopono, with tweaks I've made to it while using it with hundreds of clients and attendees at my events. The effects are profound, so only try it if you're willing to let go of *all the things* that keep you from trusting that life wants to support you and keep you from being open to receive that support.

Going into the practice, you might be thinking about all the people you need to forgive. I've got a spoiler for you: the person who needs the most love, compassion, and forgiveness is you, mama.

Forgiveness Practice:

1. Pick a topic, theme, specific person, or area of your life where you know there's a lot of pain, trauma, or energy that is keeping you stuck. For the purposes of this chapter, specifically, start with the theme of Trust. All the times and all the ways you didn't trust life, yourself, or other people, or had your trust broken.

2. Make a list of every painful, shameful, awful memory you have about it.

3. Along with each item on the list, write down every person involved in the memory (hint: you are the common denominator, so always include yourself).

4. Once your list is complete, use these prompts for each person listed and for every painful or traumatic memory:

   I forgive you...

   I'm sorry...

   Thank you...

   I love you.... (Or I send you love, sometimes we just can't muster up an "I love you" for people. That's ok, sending love works just as well.)

Another note here: although the practice is quite effective if all you do is repeat the prompts for each person, I have found that the deeper you can go into each one, and really let yourself *feel* the fullness of the pain, which you may have never let yourself do before, the more effectively you will clear it the first time through.

Some memories are so deep and painful it might take a few times to clear them, and that's normal, too. Don't judge yourself through this process. It will take what it needs to take, but that doesn't mean each time you try it isn't loosening the grip of these painful parts of your past. My friend Kate says, "You have to feel it to heal it." That's what this practice and purpose is all about.

The reason this practice works so well is that by the time you get to the "I'm sorry" piece, you become available, often for the first time ever, to see all the ways the people you're forgiving (including you), were doing the best they could. Even if their "best" at the time was really, really shitty. You get to consider all the ways you didn't know any better and they didn't know any better, observe the pain people are in, and the choices people make when they're in pain–including, perhaps yourself.

Again, I'm not saying the hurtful, abusive, or callous things people do are OK, I just want you to experience the healing of releasing the energy around it. Then, notice the beauty of filling your heart with love and compassion instead. Understanding isn't even necessary. You may never understand the *why* behind some of the things you've experienced in your life, and luckily, that's not required for you to heal it.

Once you clear out some of your negative associations and beliefs around trust, you will be much more open and available for receiving, which we'll get to in a minute. Choosing trust consistently turns your soul's voice into a fact. It *almost* eliminates that pesky old habit of overriding that innate wisdom with your logical mind. I say "almost" because you're human, and of course you'll forget sometimes. The key is to *remember* more often than you forget.

In the *Untame Yourself* book companion, I've included a video demonstration of this practice with a few examples, so you can be super clear on how it works before you do it.

Visit untameyourself.com/companion to download it now.

Foundations for Receiving

The first foundational step toward receiving is trust, which we just covered. Trust opens you up. If you're closed off, you can't receive. Imagine a basketball hoop that has a cover on it. You can shoot hoops all day, but you're never going to make a shot while the lid stays on. Same goes for receiving! If you're closed off, you can ask, hope, or wish for things as often and as emphatically as you can–but you're never going to get them consistently.

An *open heart* filled with love, trust, and compassion is a soft place to land, and an available vessel for receiving.

The next step in receiving your desires is *active appreciation*. Want more great things in your life? Practice putting attention on what you've already got, so it can expand. Good energy is magnetic, and it wants to expand and attract more of itself. The best way to practice this is to grab your journal and appreciate all over it.

Here's a prompt you can use (and a great option for the four minutes of journaling in the 9-minute morning ritual I gave you in Part I):

Make two columns on your paper: one labeled **me**, another labeled **life**. Under each column, list out *every single, possible thing* you can appreciate right now about yourself and your life.

Here are some thought-joggers if you need help getting started:

- Things people thank you for most often

- Things that come naturally to you

- Any compliments you've been given recently

- Anything you secretly or not-so-secretly like when you look in the mirror

- The things or people in your life that make you feel good, happy, loved, abundant, or satisfied

- What or who makes you laugh, supports you, or enjoys your company the most

Create additional prompts in the spirit of these.

Once you finish that list, take a moment to reflect on how it felt. Was it easy for you? Hard? How so? Did you want to judge yourself or play down your strengths?

Minimizing your strengths is totally normal. Our culture often encourages and preaches confidence, self-esteem, and gratitude, but once you start to live it out loud, people who aren't doing so, who aren't genuinely having a similar experience, may feel threatened, or react negatively to your expressions, your behavior, your truth. *It's not your job to protect others from having their hard feelings.* Your job is to shine.

Marianne Williamson says in her famous quote: "When you shine your own light, unconsciously you give other people permission to do the same." I created a whole campaign around this in 2014 called #ishineyoushine based on shared celebration, uplifting stories, and a community for honoring all that is good and brilliant about you and your life.

(I also re-run #ishineyoushine about once a year. If it sounds like something you'd like to participate in, get on the notification list here so you get an email the next time I do it: http://untameyourself.com/shine)

If you're going to receive everything you want in life, you've got to get comfortable shining brightly as the sun, and honoring all of your blessings, gifts, and talents. It helps to know this: one light cannot dim another, so turn it up, woman! TURN. IT. UP.

To bring this back to receiving, have you ever seen moths all hovering around a lamp? Imagine you're the lamp, and the moths are like all your dreams and desires. Turn up the light and watch it all come in with ease, grace, and abundance.

Believe and Receive

The last foundational part of receiving is adopting the belief that you are always in the right place at the right time, surrounded by everything you need.

Remember back when we covered mantras? Here's this belief in mantra form: "I am exactly where I need to be, surrounded by everything I need."

Since your thoughts become beliefs, and those beliefs bring things into material form in your life, using that mantra every day can certainly speed up the process of getting what you want.

Active Receiving

Now that you've got the foundational pieces in place, you're ready for the *active* part: engaging in the steps you can take whenever you want to call something in and get it.

I'll give you an example of how it works, and then break down the steps to show you the decisions, choices, and practices in detail.

In the spring of 2015, my friend Angela shared in a Facebook post that she has a vision for totally unwavering excellence in her life, and no tolerance for mere adequacy. Socks with holes get trashed immediately, and she upgrades to fresh socks–cashmere, even. Anything broken or not 100% satisfactory–she upgrades it.

And she mentioned that when she started living like she was earning $100,000 each month (instead of waiting around for it to happen first), it wasn't very long before she *had* her first $100,000 month.

That same day, I looked at my phone, which had started doing weird things like letting me text some people and not others, screen-freezing and other unpleasantness. I upgraded to an iPhone 6, a 64 GB version.

Then I thought about my upcoming trip to Austin, TX, to attend a business mastermind event. The host of the event sent a list of hotels to choose from ranging in price and level of luxury, and I felt inspired (but nervous) to book my stay at one of the nicer places. I'd normally try and find a cheaper deal, or an Airbnb, but I thought of Angela saying, "Adequate? Screw that."

My total stay was six nights, so I looked up how much it would cost to book the nicest accommodations and it made me really doubt myself. It started raising all the questions in my mind. *Is this a waste? I never spend this kind of money on travel. Who do I think I am? I don't need this. Blah blah blah....*

Rather than be impulsive about it, I decided to ask for some Divine support. When I ask for things, I always write them out, as this practice makes it feel more *real* to me (similar to how I write out my prayers as mentioned earlier).

Here's what I wrote in my journal:

DIVINE REQUEST FOR A SIGN ->

I want to follow the inspiration Angela offered, to have no tolerance for 'adequacy' and to live like I earn $100k per month. If I am to stay at the nicer place for my entire Austin visit, please show me loudly and clearly that it is so. What I need to feel is full, abundant, safe, and cared for. Alternatively, I want to feel completely awestruck at how obvious it is that I should book this stay. I would love to decide by Friday 3/13. If I don't perceive the sign by then, I will make another arrangement. Thank you!

Then I played the "I wonder..." game, which I learned from Sonia Choquette when I interviewed her for my podcast. It's her way of engaging with your intuition, or accessing your body's wisdom. What you do is place your hand on your heart, say, "I wonder..." and fill in the rest of the sentence with whatever arises. Here's what mine looked like that day:

I wonder if it will look like a gift? Some unexpected money? A new client? A retreat spot filled? An investor proposal?

And you know what happened? Not even two hours later, I got an email that I earned an extra $3000 I wasn't expecting. Awe struck: *check*. Obvious: *check*.

Unexpected money – *check*.

So I booked the luxury stay, celebrated with myself, and thanked the Divine for working so quickly on my behalf and for always having my back.

Now before I recap how this works, I want to pause and make sure you know that this works for all kinds of things, not just money. I know conversations around money can be triggering for some. This one example just happened to be around money and lifestyle upgrades.

The Steps

1. **Ask for what you want.** This can be guidance, a sign, or a specific thing. Write it out, being clear and specific not just about what you want, but *how* you want it or need it to feel if you're to say Yes to it, or how you will recognize it as having come to fruition. This is important, because to break away from the conditioning of "small thinking" that most of us have, we have to get used to seeing what we are not as accustomed to looking for. It's kind of like the difference between imagining or setting up a regular photo and the panoramic view.

Switch your setting to panoramic, and watch your life improve immensely.

2. **Wait with joyous expectancy.** This does not mean passivity. "Wait" is a verb, meaning you get to take some action here on your own behalf, which may include visualizing it. Imagining how you'll feel when your thing or your Divine guidance or support arrives. Will you squeal with delight? Tell somebody? Fist pump? Do a dance? Actively engage with "producing" the mental movie of getting what you want, and have fun with it. Again, your investment of energy can make a crucial difference in the experience you have.

3. **When you get your sign or whatever it is you asked for, *celebrate* it and *thank* the Divine.** Not just mentally, but take time to really feel the fullness of having your wants, needs, or desires met. Feel the immense pleasure of support. One of my favorite celebratory phrases is "Yes please, more of this!!"

4. **Take action upon your sign and claim it.** This is where that critical choice of *trust* comes back in. I know there will be temptation, when you get what you asked for, to talk yourself out of receiving it. You will have many ways to rationalize that: it's too easy, you have to work for it, you don't deserve it when other people are suffering, it's too good to be true, etc. Don't deny yourself this gift, the proof that the Divine sees and supports you. This is all a part of the old conditioning we've all had. Take a moment to notice resistance if it comes up, then let it go. *Accepting* is part of receiving. It's how we show the Divine that we want more, that we're ready, open, and willing to receive.

One final note for you: if this is something you've never done before, give it a try on something small at first. It can even be something like, "What do I want for lunch today?" This practice is like building a muscle at the gym. You're not going to start out with the heaviest weights. That would be demoralizing–and inappropriate. Start where you feel safe and comfortable asking for guidance and receiving, and then progress from there.

IV.

COMMUNICATING & RELATING

CHAPTER TEN
Transparent Communication

Before we dive in, I want to make a brief case for transparent communication, calling in part on the wisdom of Brené Brown, whose teachings on shame and vulnerability have greatly shaped my practices and approach:

Our culture teaches us about shame—it dictates what is acceptable and what is not. We weren't born craving perfect bodies. We weren't born afraid to tell our stories. We weren't born with a fear of getting too old to feel valuable. We weren't born with a Pottery Barn catalog in one hand and heartbreaking debt in the other. Shame comes from outside of us—from the messages and expectations of our culture. What comes from the inside of us is a very human need to belong, to relate.

Transparency is not only crucial, it's healing—because it kills shame. Shame cannot survive in the light, because it is dissolved by empathy. When you are in the practice of open, loving communication, events, thoughts, and things that could fester and grow under a cloak of shame get to come out of hiding and resolve themselves.

Transparency breeds ease

The definition of transparent is: easy to perceive or detect. Key word: *easy*. There's a show called "Kids Say the Darndest Things" that's really funny and entertaining. What's interesting, though, is how often the kids are just telling the truth, or certainly the truth as they can see it.

As adults, we've learned so many sneaky tricks for hiding our feelings or protecting ourselves and each other. We tend to get away from our original, childlike way of being–when we just told the truth. Sometimes we tell ourselves we're being tactful, but really, we're withholding. This chapter is about being open and truthful in an adult way, one that doesn't have to be abrasive or offensive, and one that will create more connection, intimacy, and ease in your relationships.

The areas where people have problems with transparent communication come down to two broad categories: what you say, and what you don't say.

At some point or another, most women receive feedback that we're too sensitive or emotional. Maybe you've been called "crazy" or even, "a bitch." Maybe it was in some small way deserved, but most of the times that criticism flew out, it probably wasn't even close to being true. Regardless, you believed it anyway.

We let lies into our minds and hearts like:

"No one can or wants to handle the full range of my emotions."

"I'm too much."

"I should tone it down."

"I shouldn't feel this way."

These thoughts take up residence in our psyches, and we start to modify our behavior accordingly. We do things that get us out of integrity with ourselves (and others), like bury our emotions and completely deny them. Sometimes, we downplay and withhold our true feelings, and try to just deal with it on our own.

I used to be really good at this. I would block things out, talk myself out of feeling things, make excuses for people to convince myself their behavior was tolerable, and choose to (*pretend to*) "feel better" about it. It was pretty bad, and I finally recognized it after my last breakup. There was a moment in the breakup conversations when my ex mentioned not feeling completely "in it" for several months. This was true for me also, but neither one of us ever said anything!

Even though I believe everything happens for a reason, I'd be lying if I didn't admit to feeling like we wasted at least six months of our lives in an unfulfilling relationship because of our unwillingness to be transparent. After it ended, I promised myself I would never do that to myself anymore. I would only commit to a man who could and would stay present with me through any range of emotions, a practice that would require me to be honest, open, and real about my feelings even when I felt afraid.

Transparent communication means being honest without being irresponsible or immature with your emotions, whether you communicate with others, or with yourself.

How It Works

Transparent communication is not for sissies. It can be risky business. The reason I say so is that it's so far from the way most of us have learned to communicate that you're bound to be a bit clunky with it at first. Also, just because you're being open and honest doesn't mean other people will follow suit right away. Just keep going. It gets easier and you get better.

It starts with you, of course. (I'm sure you're not surprised about that at this point, are you?)

Being completely honest with yourself about how you actually feel, and totally clear about what you want out of your relationships is key. I'm not promising clarity alone will get you exactly what you want. When you're honest and clear with yourself, you can speak up more effectively and consistently for yourself. That means you're more likely to have satisfying experiences and make faster progress in every endeavor.

Another helpful practice is to release yourself from the need to be understood, and, conversely, to also release yourself from the need to understand others. You don't need to understand people to accept them. I learned one of my favorite life lessons from my mom at a very young age: "To each their own."

Agreeing to disagree is one of my favorite strategies for relating to people. There's a saying: "Would you rather be right or happy?" Um... happy every time, thanks! Plus who has the energy to try and understand the perspective or motives of every mofo on the planet you disagree with?! I'd way rather just let them be and love them anyway. The need to be right is one of the biggest energy sucks out there, and it is totally avoidable.

Happiness and freedom come far more easily by disentangling yourself from these common perception and validation traps.

The next key is identifying expectations you have for the relationship–you can do so for any or each family, professional, romantic, or other significant relationship in your life. Most of the conflict we create evolves from unmet expectations. Some of your expectations are conscious–meaning you're well aware of them. Others are unconscious, meaning you don't even know they're at play. A simple practice for identifying these is to *question your hot buttons*. This is a little like the thought work I talked about in Part II.

What I mean by that is, when something upsets you, i.e., "pushes your buttons," check yourself before you wreck yourself. Before you have any emotional reactions or say something you don't mean, ask yourself, "What are my expectations here? Of myself? Of others? Why am I expecting this?"

I highly recommend writing these down, since it's always helpful to get things out of your head and onto paper, where you can review them with fresh eyes when you're not feeling them. This gives you the ability to objectively evaluate who you need to communicate with, or to consider whether your expectations in this situation are even valid. Perhaps it's you who needs to adjust accordingly.

Even though taking the time to pause and reflect sounds so simple, don't underestimate the significant difference it makes.

Sometimes you may realize the conflict isn't a big deal and let it go before it can even turn into an issue. Other times, it needs your attention and effort, because it *is* real and probably solvable. When you don't communicate your expectations, you relinquish your right to complain or be upset. People can't read your mind.

I had a client like this once. She had all these expectations of her family members and how they should be doing things, from making life choices to chores around the house, but didn't always let them know what those expectations were. When they didn't do things her way, she'd get angry. Even when they did comply, she'd still find something wrong with the results. So this was a double whammy: she was harboring both uncommunicated *and* unreasonable expectations. Living with her was no fun–and she knew it. She didn't want her family to have to walk on eggshells around her anymore, and she didn't want to continue feeling disappointed by them all the time.

Eventually, I helped her let go of her need to have everything done her way. We also worked toward communicating her new, more reasonable expectations clearly, so her family could either comply, or opt out of the attempt and find an alternative solution instead. She got more comfortable with the idea that "done is better than perfect," and realized that her way wasn't the *only* way. Her family still didn't always get things perfectly in her eyes, but she no longer needed them to–and *everyone* felt better.

Being honest about what you expect or desire doesn't always mean you're going to get your way, but you will always feel better after being open than you will when you continue holding it in or feeling unspoken disappointment. Your honesty will also inspire others around you to open up about their needs or expectations as well. Your skills at communicating transparently will also model a better way for everyone you relate to–

although this will not always be comfortable, it opens the door to healthier dialogue and potentially inspires others to grow, too.

When everyone's cards are on the table, you may not have complete control, but you do have a much healthier influence over what happens–because you're operating from total truth and transparency, no hiding or holding back.

Quick caveat here: once you identify your own expectations, you might initially feel ashamed or embarrassed of the ones you were less conscious about. That's just residue of your old programming, usually the common belief of "not getting to want what you want." You're allowed to want what you want now–and you deserve to get it, too. Whether or not you get it however, does *not* determine your self-worth. The fact that you are courageous enough to ask for it, or take action toward it, does.

Set agreements

Agreements are how you systematize your relationships and the communication norms within them. I get that the word "systematize" might not sound or feel very sexy. Yet the results–repeatable, predictable outcomes from your words, actions, and behavior–those are sexy and feel *really really good.*

Not having to analyze things over and over or repeat frustrating patterns? Sexy.

Less error and conflict? Ssseeexxxxyyy.

More love, openness and ease? Yes, please.

And this goes back to our earlier discussion of masculine and feminine. Structure creates freedom. Containers make it safe for free-flowing expression to happen inside of them. This is why the effort will be worth it.

Here are some examples of agreements I've had with romantic partners in the past:

- When one person cooks, the other person cleans.

- Regarding affection, snuggling or holding hands with other people is okay, but any sexual contact, including kissing or touching of breasts or genitals, is not.

- No one posts anything on Facebook about the other person without their consent.

The great thing about agreements is they give you focal points to return to and eliminate gray areas. You can always revisit them and make adjustments depending on what's going on and how you and the people you share them with are feeling, or if your needs, wants or desires within the relationship change.

This method is really effective in other contexts, too.

- Molly works from home two days a week. She has an agreement with her boss to check in at some point in the afternoons, when she's not in the office, to make sure they're both in the loop on their current projects.

- I used to always get off the phone with my mom as quickly as possible if I could tell she wasn't in a good mood when she answered. She later shared with me that she felt bad when I did that, and asked me to just see if she needed anything instead. She doesn't actually need me to do anything for her, she just appreciates being asked, so I do.

I could continue listing examples, but I trust you get the point. Agreements are the jam!

In case you're worried about how to establish Expectations and Agreements in your own relationships, I've got a whole framework for you that will make it as painless as possible. You can find that in the next chapter (but don't skip ahead!).

Expectations and agreements are not the only components to transparency, they're just really foundational and common ones. Transparency is about sharing anything you normally wouldn't, especially once you've paused, felt into what's really happening behind the feelings for you, and feel ready to share. I call this kind of sharing having a courageous conversation. This is also covered in the next chapter.

The biggest, fattest "what if"

A question my clients ask me all the time when we talk about transparent communication: "What if I offend someone?"

Here's my take on *being offended*. Like many other things you may not have regarded as a choice before, being offended is a choice, too. When you feel offended, it's often because you're taking something someone said or did personally, when it doesn't actually have anything to do with you. This doesn't mean you're not allowed to have hurt feelings, this is, however, an invitation not to hold on to them for too long.

Other people's words and actions may be directed toward you, but it's never entirely about you. It's always mostly about the person delivering the feedback. There's a great quote by Anais Nin to remember in this context: "We don't see things as they are, we see things as we are."

I love this quote because it also compels us to have more compassion for people. For example, when you hear negative or judgmental words that others are using to describe you, instead of feeling offended or taking them personally, have compassion because you understand that "if you spot it you got it." This means whether or not their words accurately describe you, they do accurately describe them. Feedback from other people is often more like confessions of their own stuff, perspectives, experiences, and opinions than it is about us—especially if we are not sharing transparently what *is* about us. When we get negative feedback, we often struggle to contain our reactions. Again, check yourself before you wreck yourself. Is this really about you, or is this someone else's matter entirely? Is it based in the truth? Or have you withheld important information that's contributed to the formation of someone else's hurt feelings or reactions?

With the energy of love and compassion behind your communication, you've done everything you possibly can on your part to be considerate of the other person's feelings. If they are still offended, that's on them. It's not your job to take responsibility for other people's feelings.

CHAPTER ELEVEN
The Courageous Conversation

If anyone were to ask me, "Hey Elizabeth, what's the most life-changing chapter of your book?" I'd probably say this one.

Before we get into the instruction, I'll tell you about two of the courageous conversations I was most afraid to have since I started having them. The first was with an old boyfriend. We'd been living together for about seven months, and I was still having a hard time adjusting to living with a partner (it was my first time). It finally dawned on me that one of the biggest reasons I struggled is because for over a decade, wherever I'd lived, even with roommates, I had had my own space. At least my own room. When we moved in together, even though we have a spare room, we, like most couples, decided to share the master bedroom and left the other room open for guests, and also, in our case, for movement and meditation.

That's what happy couples are *supposed* to do, right? Sleep in the same bed?

According to the models I grew up with, yes. But what if you really love your partner yet need more personal space? That was the situation in which I found myself.

I had what felt like a crazy idea to move into the guest room. The reason I was scared to bring it up is that in my experience, any couple I'd ever known who didn't share a bedroom either had problems or were kind of just mailing it in.

When I brought it up with him, I opened the conversation by saying, "Hey, can I share something with you that I'm really afraid to share but feels super important?" Of course he said yes. Then I presented my idea to move into the guest room.

At first, he questioned whether it was a good or bad thing that I felt that way. Were we breaking up? What would people think? Then he felt into the idea of sleeping on his own most nights, with the option to have "sleepovers" whenever we want. Within a few minutes, he was just as sold on the idea as I was.

Within hours, I had my clothes in the guest room closet, the air mattress set up in there. I ordered a luxury foam bed topper to make it more comfy until I set up a real bed.

So much of the desire between us that had dulled because we live and work at home–and spend so much freaking time together as a result–was allowed to return. In our case, *not* sleeping together every night created some space, mystery, and longing.

Shortly after, my partner described the new set up to someone like this: "I wake up in the morning now and I miss her, instead of looking over and thinking, 'ah, you again.'"

Had I not spoken up, who knows what my overwhelmed feelings and need for space could have snowballed into–resentment, anger, or at least tension that would have interfered with our connection.

So that's the basis for courageous conversation.

Having these open conversations with the people closest to you will create opportunities for you to practice a lot of what we've discussed throughout the rest of the book–practices around choice, allowing other people to have their own experiences, not being offended, and more.

Getting Started

When I started consciously and intentionally having these kinds of courageous conversations a few years ago, I dove right in with one of the most challenging people in my life, my mom. I say it was challenging because our beliefs at the time were so different, and because there was a lot that had gone unsaid between us for many years.

I can't speak for her, but I was reluctant to be open because I was scared to upset her, add more stress to her life, or disappoint her. I had a lot of guilt around disagreeing with her, and back then I still felt indebted to her for all the support she'd given me my whole life, almost like I thought I owed it to her to honor her opinions and feelings over my own. That wasn't serving either one of us, though.

I remember so many vivid details of our first courageous conversation. I was living in Laguna Beach, and I decided to go for a walk while I called her. Walking and talking is something that really soothes me, it's almost like movement coaxes the words, thoughts, and true feelings out of me more naturally and easily than if I were sitting. I take client calls like this all the time for the same reason. The movement also serves to keep me out of my head and present in my body to my sensations, my felt experience.

It was kind of overcast outside as I walked down the beach that day, letting the power and energy of the ocean fuel my courage, keep my heart open, and enable me to not shut down my feelings. I was pretty nervous and even had a bit of a stomachache at first. I covered almost three miles walking during our conversation. At the end, I knew everything was OK as my mom said, "Even though a lot of what you just said was hard to hear, I can feel your love and I appreciate it."

With that, we began a healing journey that we've been on together ever since. I'm never afraid to say anything to my mom anymore, and I am constantly and pleasantly surprised with how open she is and by her wisdom, and receptivity. I'm pretty sure she was always like that; I just had never given her the chance to be that way with me, or taken the time to allow myself to see her that way.

That's just one benefit of having these conversations—people can and will surprise you all the time. So much of what you fear is 100% made up in your very own mind. The only way out of that is through questioning and experimenting. Courageous conversations give people the opportunity to show you who they really are. Then, based in reality—in what's actually been said, what's actually happened—you get to decide how to move forward. No more decisions or hurt feelings that are based on made-up thoughts, theories, judgments, or expectations.

This is heaven on earth!

The Conversation Framework

The general path a courageous conversation will take includes the following elements in this rough order:

- Pre-conversation journaling

- Set up/schedule the conversation

- Intro the actual conversation

- Share don't want/afraid that

- Share do want/desired outcome

- Describe your experience

- Ask if they have anything to share

- Make your ask/present your solution

- Establish expectations/agreements, boundaries, or how you both want to do things differently moving forward

Pre-Conversation

Get clear with yourself first. Answer the questions below in your journal or the designated worksheet in the downloadable companion to this book.

- What's going on with this person that isn't OK with me right now?

- What are the things I'm feeling that I don't want to feel?

- How do I *want* to feel in relationship with this person?

- The thing I'm most afraid to say to (friend, family member, partner, co-worker, etc.) is...

- What I don't want to happen is... (What I'm afraid of is...)

- What I do want to happen/My desired outcome is...

Helpful follow-up questions to consider here build on this change or outcome:

- What support do I need?

- What change am I trying to create?

Sometimes, in the heat of a moment and loaded with fresh emotion, we say things we don't mean. Taking the time to get clear and honest with yourself ensures you only say things you truly mean, from a place of considered feelings, clarity, and calm.

Answering these questions will give you the language to use in your conversation. Don't worry, you don't have to say anything exactly the way I do, and you may not choose to share all of the thoughts or exact words in your journal aloud. You may even write it alone in your journal with no one reading over your shoulder. By starting with the full set of questions, you'll get the full truth from yourself in order to begin. No hiding.

Setting Up the Conversation

Depending on who this conversation is with and your relationship with him or her, you may want to set it up ahead of time. You might be able to just bring it up while you're together sometime soon. It's your call. This section assumes you're scheduling it in advance.

In one of his bits, my favorite comedian Dave Chappelle describes how "every man" feels when his wife or girlfriend says, "We need to talk." He only uses one word: "FU-U-UCK!!"

This doesn't just apply to men, though. A lot of us (humans) are wired to immediately assume something is wrong when someone asks, "Can we talk?" You want to be received fully, and have the person you want to talk to show up to the conversation without feeling dread, worry, or assuming the worst. That said, be sure to have the conversation in a place where you can both feel safe. A crowded Starbucks or other public place might not be the best choice. Make sure you have privacy and give yourself and the other person dignity.

Here's a script for actually setting it up (this can be a text or email if you want, but the actual conversation needs to be a real conversation, over the phone or in person):

"Hey (name), I've been working on some personal stuff lately, and there are a few things I'd love to share with you. Would you be up for a chat? Nothing's wrong, I'm just noticing some areas where I'd like to show up better, and respecting that, I would really value your thoughts and feelings."

This works well because you're taking ownership, making it about you and not them, making sure they know nothing is *wrong*, and expressing that you value their input.

Step-by-Step Conversation Script

The only reason I'm giving you a script is to reduce your opportunities for overthinking this, especially at first, while you're learning. You obviously don't have to follow this verbatim. In fact, I encourage you to make it your own. This just gives you the model so you can get to the conversations without worrying so much about what to say.

1. **Open up:**

   "Thank you so much for taking the time to chat with me, (Name), it means a lot. Like I mentioned, I've been working on some personal stuff lately, and there are a few things I'd love to share with you. Nothing's wrong, I'm just noticing some areas where I'd like to show up better and would really value your thoughts and feelings.

   "Here's what's going on..."

2. **Share your fears, don't wants, do wants, and desired outcome:**

   "I'm a bit nervous/afraid to share this with you, because I don't want (insert thing you don't want to happen, thing you're afraid of). What I do want is (insert thing you do want to happen, your desired outcome)."

3. **Describe your experience:**

I can't fully script this out for you, because I don't know what your situation or experience is. Here are some useful prompts to navigate your way through sharing your experience in a way that–this is important–doesn't blame them, shame them, or make them wrong. Your goal is simply to clearly communicate what's going on with you.

Whatever the issue or experience you're addressing is, describe:

- What feels good about it, and what doesn't?

- What's making you comfortable or uncomfortable?

- What do you want to be available for, or no longer want to be available for?

- What hurts your feelings?

- How do you want to feel?

- What do you never want to feel again?

- What have you been doing? (This is a great place to bring up expectations or introduce the idea that you are trying to change some part of yourself.)

- What do you want to do differently?

4. **Be as specific as possible.**

Again, you make this all about you in this conversation. Start addressing behaviors or scenarios with the other person, instead of attacking their character. Use statements like:

- "When this happens I feel..."

- "My feelings get hurt when..."

- "When you say things like... I assume it means..."

- "I realized I've been having an expectation that..."

What tends to happen here is a lot of "I had no idea!" moments where someone will see the impact their words and actions are having. Then, when they respond, you will very often see how the way you have felt about things was not a result of their intention at all. You are opening up so much space for new intimacy, connection, compassion, and even understanding.

5. **Thank them for listening and ask if they have anything to share:**

   "How is all of that landing for you?" or "What's present for you after hearing all of that?"

   As they answer you, LISTEN. Like, really listen. Hear what they are saying, keep your heart open, breathe, and remember not to take anything personally.

6. **Make your ask/present your solution:**

   "I'd love to share what I'd like to experience *instead* now, hear what you'd like to experience instead, and come to an agreement that feels good to both of us, cool?"

   And go from there.

How to Say No with Grace

This is a framework of its own and it's much simpler. The reason it's simpler is because you're no longer going to explain yourself to people when you say no. Often attributed to Anne Lamott, there is something you can repeat for yourself when you're having trouble with this.

"No is a complete sentence."

Now, I'll admit I giggle as I sometimes fantasize about responding to some of the emails I receive with one word, "No." That wouldn't feel good for most people to receive, and my goal when I say "no" to people is that it feel just as good as if I'd said "yes," because it's wrapped in love and approval.

The reason it's not necessary to explain yourself, though, is that it's just a waste of energy. Moreover, it often gets misinterpreted and causes more conflict. Think about it. Did you ever have someone say "no" to you with a big elaborate explanation, and you left feeling like they just totally made up an excuse? Wouldn't you have preferred to skip the excuse and just get the answer?

This always reminds me of that scene in the movie *Billy Madison*, where the principal gives a long, rude, and drawn-out explanation of why Billy's answer is incorrect and he responds, "A simple 'no' would have been just fine."

Let's take his advice and go with the simple no. Here's the formula:

Gratitude

+ "No"

+ Loving sentiment

= Graceful decline

For example, someone invites you to an event you can't attend:

"I appreciate this invitation so much. I have to decline. Have so much fun!"

A co-worker wants you to help out with something you don't have space for:

"Thank you for thinking of me. I don't have space for this right now. Good luck!"

And here's the email we send people when they reach out to invite me to collaborate, to interview me, or to do something else work-related I'm not available for:

"Hey (Name),

Thank you so much for thinking of me! And congrats, I know a lot of work goes into [whatever their invite/project is]. I'm a no for this. Sending lots of love and good juju for it!"

Again, I highly encourage you to use your own words, ones that feel genuine and true to yourself.

Give these things a try and let us know how they go by dropping us a line at hello@wildsoulmovement.com. We'd love to hear about your progress, even the messy parts.

If you're wanting more specific guidance about a personal situation in your life, email me at hello@wildsoulmovement.com. I may be able to recommend a workshop, event, course, or program for you if I've got anything that's a good fit for what you've got going on.

V.

IMPLEMENT AND INTEGRATE

CHAPTER TWELVE
Where to Go from Here

As I mentioned in the beginning of the book, ideas and discussion alone are useless if you don't take *action*. That means implementing and integrating what you just learned. In the purpose of this book, this is the path to embodiment.

Implementing just means putting a decision, plan, or agreement into effect. I've always been a great implementer. Integrating, which is combining one thing with another so they can become whole, isn't something I understood the value of entirely until just a few years ago.

You can implement like crazy, but without integrating, the results will be fleeting. It's the integration that creates the long-term results and enables real transformation.

Applied to our context here, integration is the *embodiment* of the concepts shown through the adoption and implementation of the full set of strategies and practices I've given you. In other words, this is how to *make it your own.*

Here are some tips for your journey and evolution, based on the experience of my clients in my individual and group programs in which I teach this material:

Do **not** try to implement everything all at once. In my experience, this is a surefire way to get frustrated, wind up in your head, feel overwhelmed again, and, as a result, risk abandoning your entire effort.

Do **choose** what resonates most, or feels like *the* most important thing you need right now and start there. You can't mess this up. Any positive, focused effort towards implementing and integrating *anything* in this book is useful as a starting point. Starting with your area of least satisfaction or most frustration helps you notice immediate results and rewards your effort.

Do **not** let a bad day throw you off track. Think of yourself as a super hero who just discovered her powers. They take some time to get used to, and sometimes they don't work as they did yesterday because you're learning. Sometimes it feels like it was all a dream, and we continue on the way we were before for a little while. That is, until we decide it felt *really good* to use that power.

Do **respect** the learning process. There are four phases of learning, also called the competence model, that are generally accepted in psychology. I originally learned by listening to an audio series called *Your Wish Is Your Command.* The first phase consists of unconscious incompetence, which only means you don't know what you don't know. You probably experienced that while reading parts of this book, or at any time you've been exposed to new ideas or new ways of doing something.

Soon, there's conscious incompetence, when you *do* know what you don't know. You may reach this stage when you begin to apply and exercise those concepts, knowing that there may be lots you have left to learn. We may be tentative and seek support often, and struggle against the temptation to go back to our old ways of doing things.

Next comes conscious competence, when you're generally adopting what you learned with reasonable success, yet your practice still requires a good amount of thought and effort. This is where we need some reinforcements and rewards to keep going, because we are still working hard and may not fully appreciate how far we have come or how well we are doing.

And finally, if you keep up the consistent effort (which you will because the results feel so damn good), you get to enjoy unconscious competence, where the ways of doing what not so long ago was very new and challenging becomes second nature. You don't even have to think about it.

As you progress through these four phases, there will be days when you feel deeply connected to yourself, safe in your body, tuned in, listening well, and trusting your soul's voice. Other days you might find yourself back in an old pattern, because you are learning. When that happens:

<u>Do **not** judge or speak harshly to yourself</u>. Investing any amount of your energy in negative self-talk, beating yourself up, or focusing on what "sucks," feels wrong, or isn't working is only going to create more of that negative experience. When you "mess up," notice that you did and appreciate yourself for even showing up. Imagine yourself doing better next time. Try again. Sorry doesn't make it better. Analysis doesn't help. Practice makes it better, and remember your *energy* is everything.

<u>Do **speak** to yourself the way you'd speak to a loved one</u>. I'll give you an example. Once, I got back into fitness after taking a few years off. I was in a cycling class one morning, and I was in Struggletown! My cardio

endurance was very low, but I was trying to keep up. I could feel my heart burning; I was breathless. In that moment, an older, less loving version of myself would have thought something like, "Damn, Elizabeth, you are really out of shape, what happened to you? You used to *teach* these freaking classes, for Christ's sake!"

But instead, I chose a mantra: "This is what I've got today." And then gave myself the kind of pep talk I would give to a loved one if they were in the same place: "You are doing your best, mama, I'm so proud of you. It's going to get easier every time, I cannot wait to see your progress. Way to show up and be here today, I love you so much, and damn it feels good to sweat. I missed this, and thank you for bringing this thing you love so much back into your life."

"Don't talk about it, be about it." – Busta Rhymes. This means, don't just talk about what you read or regurgitate it to others, make it *yours*. Anyone can read a book, adopt the lexicon, and convince themselves they're doing it. A lot of people do that. The actions don't match the talk, though. Others can be seen adopting the surface ideas without intent or the energy behind them, which means they are denying themselves the full depth of the experience. Why not live it fully?

Do be congruent. Make sure your actions match your intentions and your words. Pay attention to what you're telling yourself or others about what you're going to do, and get some accountability in place to make sure you follow through. Notice your patterns of success and your gaps. Step back and ask yourself how it's going and how it feels to practice. Puzzle through ways to make your success more likely to happen every day. There is no shame in making things *easier.*

And I'll tell you something – follow-through is not a skill that comes naturally to everyone. There is no shame in needing to be accountable to something or someone outside of yourself to take consistent action. After reading a book like this one, it may feel like you "shouldn't" need to be accountable to anyone but yourself. You know your behaviors, though, so if follow-through isn't your strength, don't waste time in that space of *shoulds* or self-judgment.

Instead, share what you're up to with someone you can trust who will fully support you. Get yourself into a community of women who are like you, working towards similar goals, or hire someone to hold you accountable. The "how" doesn't matter in this case. What's important is that you follow through on what it is you want to create, change, or transform.

You may want to meet and get together with women who live right near you! Maybe you can even create a book club, or at least share some wild and untamed girls' nights out!

Do **not listen** to the voice in your head that will try and talk you out of your growth. If you have chosen, practiced, and continued this far in this book, then this path is for you. Remember you deserve to feel at home in your body, to have a deeply loving and trusting connection to yourself, and to reap the benefits of honoring your soul's voice. Change can be terrifying sometimes, and some resistance or even rebellion can come up in response to this fear. If that happens, notice how you are feeling.

Do **feel all** your fears and resistance–and keep going anyway. This is another reason being part of a community is so helpful. Your sisters on the path are always there to talk you off the ledge of quitting on yourself, or help you puzzle through your blocks. There are some times when someone else gets to be the unwavering supporter for your personal growth, evolution, and love—and you may be called to do the same for someone else. This is why I get text messages from clients like this: "One day I will believe in myself as much as you do. But I'm glad you're around in the meantime!!!" It's a journey we chose together.

<u>Do **not** succumb to other people's pressure to remain the same or **change back** to how you were</u>. This is a natural part of growth, too. As you grow to embody what you've learned here, it will trigger some of the people around you. This isn't something you'll do on purpose. When unhappy people encounter happy people, and they aren't doing their own work, all their own insecurities come up. This might sound like something you don't want people to experience at your hands, but it's actually one of the most beautiful gifts you can give those around you, that awareness that they are doing and being less than they desire. Becoming uncomfortable is the first step in unlocking possibility.

<u>Do live without apology</u>. Establish your boundaries and then keep them. Commit to yourself and demonstrate your newfound love and acceptance for yourself and life through your actions. Let yourself be comfortable in the face of others' discomfort. That's not your creation nor is it your issue to resolve, it's theirs.

<u>Do not let it consume you</u>. If it starts to feel like "work," take a break. Give yourself some space. Remember, masculine energy is great for making things happen, and we need that penetrative, yang, forward-moving energy. It's not sustainable long-term. This practice is about developing

your yin, nourishing, being-energy, and eventually creating your ideal balance.

<u>Do remember to relax into your nourishing, yin, relaxing, soft, graceful, feminine energy regularly</u>. It doesn't have to be for very long, you can start with even a few minutes a day, or a few hours a week, and see how it goes from there. Experiment while getting to know how it feels and how to use it. Eventually it will become more natural to occupy that space and you will come to understand its place in your own composition of yourself. Balance is not always equilibrium. Your lifestyle may not enable you to spend equal halves of your time in each. That is totally OK. Be sure to have some go-to practices for a quick (or longer fix) when you find you want to center into your feminine energy. As you saw through various examples in this book, The Wild Soul Movement Virtual Program is a great option.

Try it out for free here: http://untameyourself.com/try-for-free

<u>Don't worry</u>. Worrying is like praying for what you don't want.

<u>Do have faith</u>. Faith is holding a vision of what you really want, even when the evidence points otherwise. Faith is trusting life, believing that you are always exactly where you need to be, and surrounded by everything you need. Having faith also means having patience while life does its thing on your behalf. You don't have to make everything happen yourself. You don't control the timelines or the results or the actions of others you may be influenced by along the way. Leave room for some magic and mystery.

CONCLUSION

"Many of us feel stress and get overwhelmed not because we're taking on too much, but because we're taking on too little of what really strengthens us."

MARCUS BUCKINGHAM

Whether you're feeling overwhelmed by the truths, stories, information, and practices in this book or you're ready to begin untaming yourself immediately, remember something I've said over and over:

This is a process that happens in layers. This journey, your truth, requires you to choose it every day. Don't expect to go from wherever you were before you picked this experience to fully embodied and untamed next week, just because you read this book.

Part of untaming yourself is gaining the intimate understanding of your personal energy so you can use it well and tap into the different aspects of it–powerfully and masterfully–when you need it.

Once you learn how to balance, use, and protect your energy, life gets better–and easier.

I cannot say this enough: thinking about everything in this book will not get you *any* results, yet putting the parts that feel the best into practice immediately and going from there, will.

You've got to take action. Even imperfect action. It will feel more natural and your results will be closer to your intent with time and practice.

The contents of this book are an accumulation of years of healing and personal development work I've done on myself, as well as with hundreds of clients. To keep the book simple and useful, I included some of the simplest tools and practices I encourage clients to implement. Simple doesn't always mean easy. Sometimes, getting a foundational concept exquisitely right can be rather challenging because it involves deep change. Be patient with yourself, and celebrate your progress as you go.

Remember the order of the Elements of Untaming Yourself. Start by connecting to yourself, practice listening, choose trust, and become available to receive. The elements work–if you work the elements.

You are a woman, which is not merely a lovelier version of a man. You get to want what you want, feel how you feel, tell the truth from your soul, and experience the fullness of your power and the fullness of life. And you get to be, have, and do all of that while fully honoring and respecting the experiences of those around you–without having to jump in anymore, force, control, or manipulate anything. This untamed living, this is the art, power, and freedom of womanhood. This is enjoying the dance between your masculine and feminine energies and always remembering that both are in your highest service.

The life-changing warning, or how to share and interact from your new viewpoint:

Once you start implementing and integrating what you've learned here and feeling the way it feels to love and accept yourself unconditionally, connect to your body, listen to her, trust her, and be willing to receive what you want in life with grace and ease, you're going to want to share your experience with other people. You will feel amazing, and you'll want others to experience the same. Or maybe you'll want others simply to understand why you feel so good now.

Just remember, you can lead a horse to water—but you can't make them drink. Go ahead and tell your friends or family to read the book. You may even find yourself gifting copies to all your favorite women. Aside from occasionally checking in and asking how they like it, stay out of the space of their transformation. Don't be the person who becomes holier than thou or self-righteous because you've discovered a path that feels better to you. This may not even be the path that is right for your friend, neighbor, or sister at this point in their journey.

Remember, everything you've ever needed has always been inside of you and the same is true for those around you. Be patient and enjoy your own experience. The best way to influence or inspire others is to live the hell out of your own life, and be as happy and fulfilled as you can be in so doing.

And last but not least, thank you. Thank you so much for giving yourself the time, attention, and energy of reading this book. Thank you for trusting me, opening your heart, and taking responsibility for your own life. Most people don't live that way. That's why the world is in the state it's in.

With every woman who wakes up, honors herself, and starts living from the integrity of her body's wisdom, we are benefitting the planet and the people around us in unimaginable ways. One of my teachers says, "May our practice benefit all beings." It can, it will—and it does.

If you get caught up anywhere as you implement what you've read, feel stuck, or something in the book doesn't make sense to you, email hello@wildsoulmovement.com. Whether I get to respond personally or someone from my team can help you out, we've got you, woman. In fact, it helps us, too, when you ask for help, because we can learn if there's a concept I didn't communicate well, or a need I didn't anticipate. That helps me figure out how I can better serve you in the future.

Be sure to take advantage of the downloadable book companion I've put together for you. It's basically a free course with elaborations on many points from each chapter of this book; exercises explained more thoroughly, worksheets, videos, links to relevant blogs and podcast episodes, and more, to help you put what you've read here to use in your life.

Below are all the places you can find me to stay in touch, update me on your progress, or even inquire about working together if you're left wanting to hit fast forward on your results, like a lot of women whose stories you've read in the book.

The practices in Untame Yourself will work for you if you take the time to apply them.

Big, wild, untamed love to you,

Elizabeth

STAY IN TOUCH

Podcast: wildsoulmovement.com/podcast

Facebook: https://www.facebook.com/elizabethdialto

Twitter: https://twitter.com/elizabethdialto

Instagram: https://www.instagram.com/elizabethdialto/

YouTube: http://youtube.com/lizdialto

Email: hello@wildsoulmovement.com

Free Resources: wildsoulmovement.com/resources

DOWNLOAD YOUR FREE BOOK COMPANION

As a gift to you for reading this book, I have created a downloadable companion online, including experiences to complement the exercises in this book, a few more examples and bits of guidance, and some of my favorite podcast episodes and blog posts that deal with the concepts in this volume. I also made a short list of my personal recommendations for further reading and exploration from some of my own favorite authors. Provide your email address at untameyourself.com/bookcompanion to receive your copy.

Take The Next Step...

Events and Classes: wildsoulmovement.com/events

Wild Soul Oracle Deck: wildsoulmovement.com/oracle

Wild Soul Toolkit: wildsoulmovement.com/toolkit

See when the next enrollment is for...

Unconsume Yourself LIVE Training:
wildsoulmovement.com/ucylive

Wild Soul Movement Virtual Program:
wildsoulmovement.com/join

Wild Soul Movement Teacher Training:

wildsoulmovement.com/tt

Coming Spring 2018...

The Wild Soul Learning Center...visit
wildsoulmovement.com/shop for details.

Acknowledgements

Every time I've flipped to the back of a book to devour the acknowledgments, I've imagined writing my own. My heart feels tender and achy to honor how deeply I've been loved, supported, and nurtured through every moment leading up to this one.

Family.

DiAltos. I love you so much. Thank you for supporting me through every wild adventure I've chosen and believing in me even when our views aren't in alignment, for never minding how loud I am, how hard or long I laugh, or how risky my decisions have been, and for never pretending to be anyone other than who you are. Thank you for speaking up for what you think is right, always trying to understand where I'm coming from and for challenging me constantly. You've all inspired and molded me in more ways than I think I even realize. (Please imagine us all in a DiAlto family hug in the kitchen now. Thank you.)

Mentors and Coaches

Some of you I've worked with directly and intensively, some more indirectly, but you've each contributed deeply to who and how I am: Jesse Elder, Chela Davison, Marie Forleo, Danielle LaPorte, Dr. Deb Kern, Angela Lauria, Sheevaun Moran.

People whose creative, techy and productive guidance and support I wouldn't have made it here without: Netanya Dilsaver, Rachel Pesso,

Geada Ford, Rebecca Reser, Katie Benedetto, Gilbert Bagaosian, Tina Jaro.

Friends, colleagues and acquaintances past and present who hold, support and inspire me. Some of you may be extremely surprised to see your names listed here. If that's you, please know something you did or said touched me so deeply, I couldn't not mention you.

Jen Blackstock, Lola Picket, Jon Vroman, James Wedmore, Amy Porterfield, Stu McLaren, Danielle Vieth, Kate Northrup and Mike Watts, Terri Cole, Sarah Jenks, Nisha Moodley, Jill Coleman, Jade Teta, Jillian Teta, Rochelle Schieck, Lisa Lister, Anthony Lemme, Christina Rasmussen, Renee Airya, Heather Lindemann, The Arch Angel Alumni, Amy Auset Rohn, Sabrina Bolin, Samuel Hershberger and the rest of my Gamma family, Jordan Gray, Andy Drish, davdji, Ali Shanti, Julie Serot, Mary Catherine Shurett, Kari Samuels, Meggan Watterson, Latham Thomas, Rebekah Borucki, Michael Hrostoski.

Wild Soul Women past and present...

Thank you for saying yes to journeying with me. Extra special love to Amy Saggiomo, Irene Sibaja, Adrienne Dinkelacker, Alex Fiorillo, Michaela Laughrin, Julie Wray, Ishita Gupta, Jen Sinkler, Sarah L'Hrar, Crecia Cipriano, Jennifer Mahoney, and Marisa Shearer.

Last but certainly not least–my cosmic support crew. The Divine Mother and Father, Jesus Christ, Mary Magdalene, Mother Mary, Archangel Michael and Raphael, Durga, Shiva, Lakshmi, Kali, Isis, and all the Divine Beings of Light, Spirit Guides, Animals and Angels who love and support me unconditionally. Thank you, I love you.

About the Author

Known for her raw, honest, and grounded approach to self-help and spirituality, Elizabeth DiAlto specializes in Integrative Spiritual Development and Women's Leadership. She is the creator of Wild Soul Movement and host of the popular Untame The Wild Soul podcast. She's been a teacher, speaker, coach and trainer to groups and individuals for 15+ years in three different industries.

Elizabeth works with women internationally through digital programs, speaking engagements and more intimately, through in-person intensives, retreats, workshops, Wild Soul Movement™ teacher training. She also provides higher level support to a small number of private clients who are working in big roles, on big dreams, creating massive change and innovation.

In 2013, Shape Magazine listed her alongside Dr. Oz, Ellen, Jillian Michaels, Tim Ferriss and more as a Top 30 Motivator. She has written for and been featured in Marie Claire, New York Magazine, SELF, Shape, The Huffington Post, US News and Health Report, Yahoo! News and many more. Before developing the current work she does with women, Elizabeth was a nationally-ranked Sales Rep and District Manager for Vector Marketing (with over $1 million in sales to her credit), a certified personal trainer, group exercise instructor and nutrition coach. She's a Reiki Master, has completed Energy Mastery trainings with Energetic Solutions, and is an avid student of many spiritual traditions and sacred lineages.

Aside from being a prolific creator and community builder, she's an insatiable learner and a sensualist who loves spas, bathtubs, dancing (especially salsa!), reading, traveling, spending time in nature, and she has a laugh that has been described as, "a sound bath of sunshine and JOY."